Money: An Owner's Manual

Enhanced and Expanded

A Personal Guide to Financial Freedom

By Dennis R. Deaton

Quma Learning Systems
Mesa, AZ

Money: An Owner's Manual

Enhanced and Expanded

A Personal Guide to Financial Freedom

By Dennis R. Deaton

Editors: April Price, Alan Goff

Assistant Editors: Rene Howard, Cecily Markland

Cover Design: Tamar Patchett

Typesetting: Tamar Patchett

Printed in the United States of America

Library of Congress Catalog Card Number 00-110747

ISBN 1-881840-06-9

Quuma Learning Systems

Acknowledgements

The author gratefully acknowledges the invaluable contributions made by:

April Joy Price, Alan Goff, Rene Howard, Kristin Perkins, Cecily Markland and **Silvana Longone** for editing, proofreading, research and content advice.

Tamar Patchett and **Larry Capps** for graphic design, lay-out and technical expertise.

Reece Bawden for leadership, wisdom and continual support.

Susan Deaton for being my soul's complement and "the wind beneath my wings."

Individual Responsibility

Since individual circumstances (financial and otherwise) vary widely, and because even the most conservative of money management and investment strategies entail some degree of risk, this book takes a principle-based approach. Each reader assumes full responsibility for making his or her own decisions as to whether, when and/or how to apply the material contained herein. This book is written, sold and distributed with the express understanding that neither the publisher nor the author are hereby rendering legal, accounting, or any other professional services. For specific legal, accounting, investment or tax advice, readers are advised to seek out and obtain the counsel and services of competent professionals in those respective fields.

Dedication

To Susan, April, Dave, Caleb, Olivia, Savannah, Jared, Melanie, Emma, Matthew, Katie, Jacob, Timothy, Rachel, Christian, Emily and David—my fabulous fortune.

And, to all those who sense that financial freedom has more to do with serenity than satiety.

PREFACE

While having lots of money is not necessarily a sign of genuine success, nor the lack of it a sign of failure, many of us should be more successful with money than we are. We continue to suffer the consequences of a host of self-inflicted wounds. This book intends to take the subject of money and make it manageable and profitable on a very practical plane, teaching principles and procedures for solving most of life's financial puzzles. People who will follow these recommendations will own lots of money. That alone would be significant, but this book intends to do more. It's going to keep pointing you to a higher plane, inviting you to see the deeper implications of your monetary motions.

You deserve not only what money can *buy,* you deserve what money can *teach.* Despite the pervasive tendency to equate piles of money with pinnacles of happiness, those who *only* pursue that goal inevitably find it to be a hollow pursuit, devoid of genuine satisfaction and fulfillment. Those who would settle for the "wealth of the world" at the expense of their character, their relationships, and their self-respect award themselves a monumental "booby prize." In the process of generating prodigious incomes and amassing huge fortunes, they become morally bankrupt and personally impoverished. They do not find happiness or fulfillment either on their journey or at their destination, discovering in the end that fulfillment had a lot more to do with inner furnishings than with outward frills.

In that regard money can be a wonderfully useful asset and teacher, leading us to personal breakthroughs on the pathway to authentic personal development and character. As we learn and apply correct principles of money management, we inevitably develop characteristics that promote competence in virtually every other facet of life as well. One cannot achieve and maintain wealth without eliminating procrastination from one's life, or without developing and practicing consistent levels of discipline, frugality, industry, persistence and thrift—a fairly laudable list of traits when you look at it. In summary, one cannot fully master money without developing mastery of oneself in the process.

So I extend to you a warm invitation to become a financial success while adding wealth to yourself in a host of additional ways. As you apply the principles and methods outlined in this book, you will find yourself taking more and more personal responsibility for your monetary life and will see even greater dimensions of achievement of which you are surely capable.

TABLE OF CONTENTS

Section I

CHAPTER 1

The Matter of Money

Bill should have been governor. He's bright, energetic, and honest—everything you'd want in a great leader. It would have been good for him and good for the citizens of his state. Although it was his dream, he didn't even run for office.

Karen has regrets, too. She wanted to go to medical school. She's empathetic and intelligent, and she would have made a fine doctor. She could have helped thousands of people. Medicine was her dream, but she didn't even apply for medical school.

The same thing thwarted both Karen and Bill: their perceptions about money. Neither thought he or she had the financial resources to pursue a dream. It all came down to money.

On the other hand, Tom *did* go to medical school. He works as a physician in a bustling clinic. But he's not very happy—he merely tolerates the practice of medicine. Tom became a doctor because he thought it would be a guaranteed way to make big money. As a boy, he'd noticed that the doctors in his hometown lived in the largest homes in the best neighborhoods. They drove the latest cars and they never had to worry about unemployment. After all, people get sick and injured in bad times as well as good. So Tom went into medicine, for one principal reason. He went for the money.

Mark and Sally are disappointed with their daughter's fiancé. Oh, sure, he's perceptive and personable, and he treats Sally like a queen, but he has one glaring flaw—he's practically a pauper. He works nights to put himself through school, and he lives in an apartment in the "old part of town." His parents, too, live modestly. Living in a small home in a tract subdivision, they've made no secret of the fact that they've struggled all their lives. Mark and Sally are just not sure that the young man is "good enough" for their daughter. Maybe they don't even consciously realize it, but their misgivings stem from their perspectives about money.

Not long ago I heard a six-year-old talking excitedly at a dinner table about the new boy in the neighborhood. "He's a really neat guy, Dad. You should see all the stuff he has—the latest electronic games, Superstar sneakers, and a really expensive racing bike!" He has picked up the cues quickly. Even a six-year-old has connected "neat" to *has* and *wears*. It always seems to come down to money.

CLUES

Something is amiss in our society. Despite our high per capita income, far too many of us are suffering the pains from self-inflicted wounds and the ramifications are far-reaching. Obvious is the fact that money mismanagement constitutes a principal source of marital tension and discord. One authority reports that over fifty percent of divorcing couples cited that conflict over money was the major cause for their break-up.[1] Pat B. Brian, a prominent attorney, adds:

> When one gets to the unraveling of the "Gordian knot" of marital conflict, it is found that the number one killer of marital happiness is money related. In divorce after divorce, the underlying cause is undisciplined money management.[2]

Consider for a moment the substantial toll exacted on society by our high divorce rate.[3] Now add the cost of lost productivity in the workplace. (Nothing siphons energy and concentration on the job like financial worries and marital strife.) The price tag for the hours of impaired creativity and productivity alone is enormous. But the problem doesn't end there. Calculate the associated health care costs and sick leave brought about by all this personal turbulence,[4] and even conservative estimates suggest a staggering annual drain.

For several decades the U.S. Department of Commerce's *Income and Poverty Report* has painted a sobering picture of the "graduating class"—the generation reaching retirement age. Typically, twenty-nine out of a hundred don't make it—they die before reaching their golden years. Now here come the jolts: *Sixteen* have annual incomes *below* the government's official poverty level! Thirty-five live on incomes ranging from $10,000 to $24,999, which might sound a little better until we realize that the majority of that group lives on incomes under $18,000 per year. In other words, they're essentially subsisting on Social Security alone. Eighteen enjoy an income of $25,000 to $49,999 annually, and *two—only two out of a hundred*—have yearly incomes that exceed $50,000.[5]

A U.S. Social Security Administration watch-dog organization reports that 80 percent of America's senior citizens are highly dependent on Social Security benefits for their living income. Specifically, Social Security provides *at least half* of the total income for more than 55 percent of our seniors, and provides more than one-third of the total income for over 75 percent of the senior population.[6] Based on 1997 Census Bureau data, analysts find that without their Social Security benefits *more than one-third* of the 65-and-older population would drop below the poverty line.[7] That's shocking! After working for some forty years, a huge portion of our population scrape by, living on the edge of indigence! Instead of touring the world, spending time with family and friends, and spoiling their grandchildren, they find themselves living on a far-too-meager fixed income.

All of this stands next to the fact that we live in a country of extensive personal freedom and flourishing opportunities, and most of us will have hundreds of thousands of dollars, if not several millions, flow through our pockets during our lifetimes. So why do so many of us end up pinched in an unpleasant financial vise? The answer comes down to ownership and who in reality owns whom. We don't seem to see the difference between *earning* money and *owning* money. In many ways we let money own us.

WEIGHTS AND MEASURES

With few exceptions, we unwittingly grant money more respect than it deserves. When it comes to making decisions, for example, we almost automatically defer to money, without even realizing that we're doing so.

Mom says to Dad, "I think daughter has a gift for music, and she wants to take lessons." What's Dad's first question? "How much will it cost?" And the answer determines whether daughter gets lessons, and how often and by whom. Dad says to Mom, "Son has his heart set on an Ivy League college; he wants to go to Yale." Reflexively, Mom says, "That's impossible! Yale's too expensive. He's not being realistic." Of course, moms and dads want the best for their children, but in the end money seems to know best, and makes the final decision.

Money permits or money denies. Money decides what's possible and what's not, what's realistic and what's wishful thinking. Nothing seems to be able to overrule it. Money approves or vetoes every plan, supports or squashes every dream.

Money has become the prime, if not the sole, indicator of value and success in the world. Rare indeed is the soul whose assessment of a peer is not heavily influenced by the other person's income and assets. The greater the income and properties, the greater the respect. We're not respecters of persons nearly as much as we're respecters of purses.

We even evaluate ourselves by this "standard." A good portion of our self-esteem rises and falls in direct relationship to the ups and downs of our income and portfolio. All too often we confuse self-worth with net worth, which is why people sink into depression when the stock market dives. When their portfolio loses value, they feel like they have lost value too.

We lessen ourselves when our compulsion to acquire financial assets becomes the central focus of our lives. Such disorientation leads to numerous pitfalls such as putting our careers ahead of our relationships, our "work ethic" ahead of our health, and our profits ahead of our ethics and values. The purse may prosper, but the person is impoverished. It's a pretty sad eulogy when only the accountant can stand up and say, "Here lies Social Security Number 808-77-1099, who turned in some impressive 1040 Forms."

THINKING RULES

So what is money—a faithful friend or an enemy? A servant or a drill sergeant? A blight or a blessing? Ask a few people, "Would a truckload of money solve your problems?" "Oh, yes!" they'll say, "If I had a big pile of money, I'd quit my job and leave my problems behind. I'd do all the things I've always dreamed of."

Pose another question: "Does money cause misery and problems?" "Yes," they'll respond, "Most of the evil in the world can be traced back to the lust for money. Wouldn't the world be great if we weren't haggling over cash all the time?"

Our indecision about money leads to an insecure relationship. We say it frees us. We say it enslaves us. We love it; we hate it. Why money doesn't have a complex over all this ambivalence is a wonder. And why doesn't it? Simply because money doesn't think. Money doesn't know or care if it comes or goes. It doesn't know if it's saved, squandered, spent or lost. Totally indifferent to our love or lust, money just goes on circulating around the globe, oblivious to all the emotion flaming in human hearts over its motions.

Actually, our disorientation is not money's fault. Although we seem to be doing our best to give money a persona, it really doesn't have one. When we get right down to it, money's as inanimate as a brick. It's not MONEY after all; it's only. . . money.

THE CRUX OF THE MATTER

The first key to owning money, rather than letting it more or less own us, is to admit to ourselves that money has no behavior outside our own. Money does not think, *we do* (or we're supposed to). Our dilemma is not about money, it's about us. Money only does in our lives what we cause it to do. Those of us who aren't satisfied with our financial harvest, had better look at what we're planting. Financial prosperity and monetary misery are products, each a derivative of a corresponding state of mind. When we accept this crucial point, we hold the key that opens the vault to genuine wealth and financial prosperity.

To own money—in every positive sense of the term—we've got to take full ownership of ourselves, and vow to be the solution instead of the problem.

---

1. WHYY 91FM, "Creating Financial Harmony," *Voices in the Family,* February 22, 1999, http://www.why.org/91Fm/Voices19902.html (October 19, 2000).
2. Author's notes from public address delivered by Pat B. Brian, Oct. 1986.
3. Department of Health and Human Services, National Center for Health Statistics, http://www.infoplease.com (October 3, 2000). "Nature and Nurture Affect Children After Divorce," *Health Information,* July 6, 2000, http://www.healthcentral.com/news (October 3, 2000).

NOTES

"More Americans on Verge of a Nervous Breakdown," *Health Information,* July 5, 2000, http://www.healthcentral.com/news (October 3, 2000).
"Divorce Doubles Suicide Risk in Men," *Health Information,* March 15, 2000, http://www.healthcentral.com/news (October 3, 2000).
The Cheltenham Group,"Divorce Process & Consequence: Annex 3 Statistics," *The Emperor's New Clothes,* July 1995, http://www.infoplease.com/divorce/ (October 2, 2000).
4. Ibid.
5. US Department of Commerce, *Income and Poverty Report,* 1988 – 1998.
6. Kathryn H. Porter, Kathy Larin and Wendell Primus, "Social Security and Poverty Among the Elderly: A National and State Perspective," *Center on Budget and Policy Priorities,* April 8, 1999.
7. NCPA, "Social Security Dependency," *Social Security,* http://www.ncpa.org/pi/congress/pd050799d.html (October 19, 2000). Gene Koretz, "Social Security Is Aptly Named," *Business Week,* May 10, 1999.

CHAPTER 2

The Difference That Makes the Difference

Have you ever been to a Pro-Am golf tournament to watch amateurs match skills with the professionals? You can learn a lot by attending one, and not just about golf. You can learn a lot about life, and the elements of success and failure. You can see, for example, some unknown amateur emerge from the ranks of the obscure to make a serious run at the victory. As a closet underdog myself, I inevitably find myself rooting for the "little guy." Pulling for the Davids is more fun than rooting for the Goliaths, even though the Goliaths usually win.

As I've watched skilled newcomers compete against the best in their sports, something has become clear to me. In most aspects of the game, the pros aren't dramatically superior to the amateurs. Many of the no-name contenders actually have better technique and more physical ability than the veterans. Yet the amateurs seldom prevail.

Why don't the amateurs win more often? Because athletic ability alone is not enough. The pros excel in their *mental* skills. They envision the game with greater clarity because they've "been there." They know what works in a given situation and what doesn't. This inner strength fosters confidence and poise in the clutch, giving them the winning edge. The mental difference makes all the difference.

Without the potent combination of accurate vision, concentration and confidence, at some point the amateurs waver. They become distracted by something—a poor shot, a bad lie, or someone undressing in the gallery. These distractions prove fatal. As their inner grip falters, their outer game unravels. Champions, on the other hand, have honed the mental edge, and that strength vaults them to victory.

The same principle holds true when it comes to money. Financial high achievers also benefit from a superior mind set—a potent blend of accurate vision, concentration and poise. Their inner strength sets them apart from the struggling masses. And, although the achievers come from diverse backgrounds, representing a spectrum of professions and incomes, their mind sets don't differ all that much. Their mental approach—the principles that they practice—is strikingly similar. They all follow pretty much the *same* mental map.

GETTING THE BEARINGS STRAIGHT

The good news about the map comes in two parts: One, their approach is not complex or mystical, and two, any reasonably rational person can adopt and implement it, securing the same superb results.

The first element of a powerful monetary mind-set centers on the distinction between two words or concepts. Think of the word ACQUIREMENT for a moment.

Acquirement. n. 1: The act of acquiring or obtaining. 2: The act of gaining possession, usually resulting from continued endeavor or effort.

Notice the phrase, "resulting from continued endeavor or effort." What image does that evoke? Doesn't it imply exertion? A lot of work—sustained striving—perhaps even *too much* of a good thing?

Don't get me wrong, financial freedom doesn't just fall out of the sky. There's no excellence without effort, and high achievers are definitely hardworking, industrious people. But, beware of "Acquirement Mentality." It's a pernicious malady because it's so subtle. Like the most insidious of viruses, acquirement mentality produces an epidemic of financial ills, afflicting a wide range of the population. People sense that something's amiss—that they're not really healthy—but they can't quite put their finger on what's wrong.

As though blind in one eye, people with acquirement mentality see only one side of the monetary equation—the income side. They confuse wages with wealth. They're always looking toward the next raise or their second job, erroneously thinking that a little more income will solve their problems. Everything would be fixed, they believe, if they could just make more money. Their incomplete analysis keeps them forever shackled to a merciless treadmill (all that "continued endeavor and effort"). They are doomed to achieve exhaustion before they find success.

Accelerated acquirement is not the quinine for our monetary malaria, because *insufficient acquirement* isn't the illness. In reality, most of us produce a respectable flow of cash, yet we allow it to stream through our fingers at mind-boggling rates. The world teems with people who can generate prodigious incomes but who'll never know a single day of financial peace.

A CASE IN POINT

I know of a man who learned the deficiencies of acquirement mentality the hard way. A physician by profession, he founded a medical practice in a growing community and for a time was the only practitioner in his specialty for miles around. He was a good doctor with excellent people skills, and his income skyrocketed. Within a few years, however, despite his bustling practice and the big dollars he was earning, he filed for bankruptcy. Here's the story:

In getting through medical school he accrued sizable debts that were followed by the costs and debts associated with setting up a practice. As the practice took off, and with such great earning prospects ahead, he decided to plunge into the construction of a luxurious home—one that he felt would "fit the image" of a prospering physician. He told himself that he "owed it" to himself and his wife. They had toiled like oarsmen to get through medical school, and they deserved to be compensated for their labors and sacrifice. So they took on an impressive mortgage.

Not long after, with the demand for his services increasing and the expenses of his ostensibly affluent lifestyle mounting, he decided to expand into a larger, nicer facility—a new clinic with more space, more image and more overhead. These steps were taken on borrowed money, leveraged funds and the promise of high future income, with little concern for the energy and interest costs he'd eventually pay. He had big income potential, he could write off the interest, and he could "shelter" some income from the IRS. Everything seemed so good, on paper. But in practicality he felt ever-increasing pressure to produce a robust cash flow.

With a lion's share of his income going to debt service, he often felt restricted in his spendable dollars and his lifestyle. He was tied to his practice, and even though it remained healthy, *he* was "maxing out." Under the relentless pressure, the harness he was wearing began to chafe. To ease his discomfort he proceeded to splurge on some expensive toys. He needed them "to get away from the rat race," he rationalized. Since most of his income was going to debt service, he compounded his problem by financing most of his toys.

Growing impatient with his "tight cash flow," he leaped into some speculative ventures which he called "investments." He thought by *acquiring a little extra income* he would finally get over the hump and be able to catch up on his debts and obligations. He knew he was spread thin, but the only tactic he could see was to resort to his old friend—acquirement. So he launched into these "investments" with no cushion, having even borrowed a chunk of his "venture capital."

Unfortunately, the investments failed to perform as quickly as he'd hoped, and rather than solving the problem, they compounded it. Some of his "investments" went south, requiring money to keep them viable. He hoped that the negative cash flow would be temporary and that he could write some of the damage off of his taxes.

As his cash flow descended into the negative, his medical practice suffered. Longer hours and more patients per hour became the norm. Soon, "going to the office" was equated with "another day on the treadmill." Not surprisingly the love of his profession dwindled and the quality of his care diminished. He was not the vibrant personable doctor he once was. Sensing this, some of his patients went elsewhere. This loss of patients reduced his income, which increased the pressure. You can picture the rest. Spiraling downward in a tragic tailspin, he crashed in bankruptcy.

Moral of the story: A lucrative profession and high income are not the determining factors in attaining wealth and peace of mind. They can help, but they're not the determinants.

KEY WORD, KEY MENTALITY

Financial high achievers don't obsess over their next raise or bonus, and neither do they go out and buy their next luxury based on next year's expected income. Underlying all of their monetary operations—and this is universal among them—they possess an abiding commitment to something stronger than acquirement.

Consider another word: ACCUMULATION.

Accumulation. n. 1: The act of amassing; 2: The act of gathering as into a great heap or pile.

People who have both money *and* peace of mind are not frantically huffing and puffing, shoveling dollars in the front door with careless disregard for what's going out the back. They're focused on accumulation—on gathering and hanging onto a sizable portion of their income. Habitually. Accumulation may not be glamorous, and it may not be slick, but it's sure and steady, and it beats the alternative by a long shot.

LARRY STUNS HIS BOSS

Larry worked for one of the subsidiaries of a multi-state conglomerate based in Arizona. He was good at what he did and he enjoyed his employment. As a maintenance mechanic, Larry wasn't in the upper echelons of income in his company or even his division. Yet, Larry retired early and he retired well—earlier than his bosses and better than most of his higher-paid co-workers.

Just prior to his sixtieth birthday, Larry dropped somewhat of a bombshell on his boss—a man who'd worked for the company longer than Larry, and who'd enjoyed a consistently higher income. Larry told his boss, "I resign."

His boss looked shocked. "What's the problem, Larry? I thought you were pretty happy here, and we're pleased with your work. Why are you leaving?"

"There's no problem," Larry replied, reassuring his boss that he wasn't a disgruntled employee serving his notice. "I'm retiring," he said.

The boss' expression shifted from shock to concern. "Are you sure? I mean, it takes quite a bit to retire these days. Are you going to be all right?"

"Yes, I've thought about it carefully, and I think we're going to be fine."

Larry could tell that his boss, who'd become a good friend over the years, was still unconvinced. So Larry went into detail.

"We'll be all right. Our cars are both paid for. Our home in Tempe is free and clear, and we have a vacation home up at Lake

Havasu, and it's paid for too. We own ten mountain lots, and I'm thinking of building a home on one of those lots every year and selling it. We have over $200,000 in savings, and with the retirement income from the company's 401(k) we're going to be quite comfortable. In a few years, I'll start drawing my social security and that'll be a bonus."

The boss' expression shifted from concern back to amazement. Realizing that Larry was in a much stronger financial position that he, the boss' response was, "Looks like I'm the one with the problem."

AND JACK

Jack worked for a large mining company as a common laborer for thirty years. He too retired long before his foreman, his supervisor, and even the mining superintendent. He said, "The mine paid me more than I needed, so I just kept putting a little extra away every month. I bought some of the company's stock, and it did pretty well. We've got well over a million dollars in the bank right now, and that'll last us for the rest of our lives."

These are but two of the many examples that could be cited of people who've earned rather modest incomes at the outset, but who've achieved and maintained impressive levels of personal wealth. But, unless people have the right perspective about income and cash flow, they'll struggle, no matter how much money they make.

THE LAWS OF ACCUMULATION

Now prepare for the ultimate in simplicity. Only two laws have to be mastered in order to accumulate money:

Law No. 1: Don't spend all you earn.

Law No. 2: Don't lose what you save.

We don't have to be Albert Einstein or Marilyn vos Savant to gain financial victory. We don't have to subscribe to a rack full of savvy newsletters. We don't have to graduate from Harvard, be clairvoyant, excessively beautiful or slim. What we must do is muster a little discipline, curb our lust for acquirement, and concentrate on applying the laws of accumulation and the principles that flow from them.

Neither hair color nor build, neither genetics nor gender, neither birthright nor birthplace, neither education nor occupation, not even income makes the difference. Financial high achievers have no unique identifying characteristic except one—their mind-set. They recognize the significant difference between acquirement and accumulation.

Section II

CHAPTER 3

Fallacy No. 1: Just a Little More Money Will Solve My Problems

Carlo Collodi may not have intended to write a financial allegory when he wrote *Pinocchio,* but he certainly conveyed some timeless wisdom. As you know, Pinocchio leaves home with the clear intention to repay his father for all his love and sacrifice by going to school and making something of himself. But young, naïve Pinocchio soon loses focus on that goal and falls prey to numerous enticements as deceitful hucksters separate him from his school book, his clothes, and what little money he has to support himself.

Among several useful lessons we can learn from this story is one about the importance of subordinating impulses to worthy long-range goals. Implicit in that equation is the need to set clear, accurate, long-range targets for our future. Successful accumulation and clearly defined goals walk hand-in-hand. In the absence of meaningful goals, discipline is virtually impossible, and we succumb to a "spend and hope" lifestyle (spend now and hope things work out in the future). Designing sound financial goals is essential, and we'll accomplish that step when we get to the Wealth Plan later on.

The second lesson to be learned from the Pinocchio allegory concerns becoming wise and wary when enticed by the many get-rich-quick ploys that beckon us. The path to financial prosperity is fraught with fallacies. We prepare ourselves for success when we can spot their inconsistencies and avoid the pitfalls that siphon wealth.

THE ALLURE OF MORE MONEY

The magnetic appeal of acquirement mentality arises from the seductive myth that more money, like some magic potion, can cure anything that ails us. People who hold to this fallacy believe that money will solve anything from their children's poor grades to trouble with the neighbors. "If we had a little more money, Blanche, we could build a moat around the yard, so they couldn't come onto the property any more." (Meaning the neighbors, not the kids. Or, maybe not.)

"If I had enough money, I'd tell my boss to take this job and stuff it. Then I'd do something meaningful with my life," is a familiar variation on the theme. "If we had a little more money, honey, we'd get along better. All these bills are putting so much pressure on us—we're both a little cranky," is yet another version.

More money appears to be the master magician that can make any problem—anything from a shallow self-image to a rocky marriage to a dead-end job—disappear. But it can't and it doesn't.

Interestingly, those with the strongest belief in this fallacy are those with the least amount of money. When some of us finally do obtain a chunk of money, we're surprised to discover that problems don't miraculously vanish. In many ways a lot of money actually compounds one's problems, and even opens the door to a whole new set of dilemmas. As a wealthy friend of mine put it, "Lots of money can be more of a curse than a blessing."

SURVEY SAYS

In preparation for this book we surveyed a broad range of occupations and lifestyles. The spectrum ranged from rather modest to very high incomes. The survey consisted of two questions:

(1) Do you make enough money to live comfortably each month?

Take a wild stab at the predominant answer. Almost without exception, the answer was "no." And when they spoke candidly, most people admitted to overspending their income frequently. For most, such spending was actually the norm.

The next question was even more revealing:

(2) How much more would you need per month to live comfortably?

Some people had to think about it for a moment. Others had an amount or a percentage right on the tip of their tongue. When we began plotting the responses on a graph, something immediately became apparent. A large proportion of the answers clustered around one specific percentage—ten percent.

One other trend also showed up. When the overspending exceeded ten percent, almost invariably, the culprits were from the *high* end of the income spectrum.

The whole portrait seemed to verify a maxim known as "Parkinson's Law." "Spending will always rise to meet or exceed income." In this case the word "law" is misapplied. In science the word "law" ordinarily refers to an inviolable principle of the universe—a *cause* that produces a specific, predictable *effect.* Such laws, like Newton's Laws of Motion, are the reasons why things happen the way they do in the physical universe. In the strict sense, Parkinson's Law is *not a law;* it can, and by all means should be violated. However, this pattern of overspending is so universal and consistent one might think it was an immutable law of the galaxies.

Pointedly, we're suffering from an *epidemic of monetary Parkinson's disease!* This rampant epidemic affects us individually and collectively. Congress, as you know, suffers from regular episodes of spendthrift fever. Individuals, families, or governments who habitually overspend will eventually come to a day of reckoning. Choices will be limited. Prosperity will diminish. The shackles slip on lightly and easily. Once in place, however, they clamp down tightly. After that, only concerted effort and persistence can free us.

Some folks love to harangue the government for all its deficit spending, but it all boils down to the fiscal integrity of "we the people." Many of us, who'd jump on the bandwagon to deplore the spending habits of Congress, need to inspect our own houses. Can we legitimately decry deficit spending by our senators while we, ourselves, live on credit cards? In a keen twist of irony, we find that our *representatives* do in fact *represent* us! All they're doing on Capitol Hill is what most of us do at home.

We reap as a nation what we sow at home. Fiscal irresponsibility is not about this anonymous *them out there;* it comes down to *us in here.* Our own flaws impede us, and our own strength and integrity accelerate us.

THE TOOL OR THE CARPENTER?

"Just a little more money will solve my problems" is an insidious fallacy because it's so convenient. It requires no introspection, no meaningful self-assessment and no real change in attitude or behavior. It just requires more huffing and puffing in the name of acquirement. But, money doesn't solve problems, minds do. Money is only a tool and, unless used with skill, it actually causes more damage than good. We only need to look at a few lottery winners to prove that point. The level of each "winner's" personal discipline determines whether the windfall becomes a blessing or a curse. Hitting the jackpot doesn't suddenly transform freewheeling spendthrifts into financial geniuses.

As a general rule, we find more stress and worry among high earners than among those who earn less—at least the ones who haven't seen through this fallacy. Some of them are digging holes for themselves (how about, canyons) at breathtaking speeds. They are heavy with debt, heavy with worry, and heavy with anxiety about the future. When I let some of my modest-income friends in on this observation, they seemed to experience no end of satisfaction. All these years they had been thinking that their high-income friends were carefree spenders. They are liberal spenders all right, but most of them are far from carefree. They toss and turn at night, fretting over debts, bills and cash flow.

A LAW WITHOUT EXCEPTIONS

More money doesn't rectify our flaws, it magnifies them. This precept holds true because a law of the universe does exist and, unlike Parkinson's Law, that law does apply without exception. I call it "The

Inescapable Law of Appetites, Passions and Lusts", and here's what it states:

> Spending money on appetites, passions and lusts will *intensify* them rather than *satisfy* them.

Unless and until we subdue our appetites, passions, and lusts, we will *never* have enough money. The shortest distance to wealth and prosperity is a straight line called self-discipline.

CHAPTER 4

Fallacy No. 2: You Gotta Buy When They're Low, Sell When They're High

Financially successful people invest. They don't speculate or gamble. On the "List of Financial Fallacies", none is more important to grasp than this one. Investing and speculating are not twin brothers. They're not even first cousins. They come from totally opposite mind-sets—180° apart. Speculators use the word "invest," but they are actually engaged in an entirely different pursuit. Speculation is a particularly arrogant version of acquirement mind-set we'll call "prospectors' mentality."

Prospectors' mentality blends a little greed with a little pride and comes out sounding something like this. "I am an exception in the universe. The laws that apply to others do not apply to me. Other poor stiffs will have to toil for years, but I'm smart enough to find the quick route to riches."

A MONUMENT TO PROSPECTOR'S MENTALITY

Not far from my home in Arizona (I can see it from my east windows right now) there looms a formidable geological feature.

Called "Home of the Thunder God" by the Apaches, this jagged remnant of molten matter now goes by the name "Superstition Mountain." Legends about this unusual peak abound. Perhaps you've heard of the Lost Dutchman's Gold Mine—a vein of rose-colored quartz infested with gold nuggets that lays hidden on or near Superstition Mountain. The story has roots dating back to the 1800s.

Over the decades, thousands of hungry souls have come to Superstition Mountain hoping to cash in on quick riches. Each believed that he or she was destiny's child and would be the one—the lucky prospector to stumble onto the lost trove. Some enterprising chaps have even made good livings selling "the one and only true map to the Lost Dutchman's gold mine." Spinning stories about Apache secrets and old prospectors making deathbed confessions, they've duped the gullible into paying jaw-dropping sums for totally bogus maps.

This monument to prospectors' mentality has seen hundreds of people work for decades, pounding on the rocks, sleeping on the sand, sifting the dirt—believing that at any moment Luck or Fate would grant them sudden riches. All to no avail.

SAME PLOT, DIFFERENT STAGE

As a means of getting rich quick, Superstition Mountain is not unique. Lately, a fair number of people have gone prospecting in faster, easier ways. They don't sleep on the sand or sift any dirt. They just walk into a convenience store and "play" the lottery. (How the verb "play" became associated with handing over a buck to a cashier is beyond me.) The nice part about this type of prospecting is that we don't get all that dirt under our fingernails. But the *mentality* is the same. People who play the lottery tell themselves that the gargantuan odds that apply to everyone else don't apply to them. "You can't win, if you don't play" goes the rationalization, ignoring the fact that mathematically the chances of winning the lottery are precisely the same *with* or *without* a ticket.

In other examples of prospectors' mentality, the props differ but the plot stays the same. The spirit of speculation is the spirit of prospecting dressed in a business suit. People hear tales of somebody's friend or relative, or friend of a friend's relatives (it doesn't really matter, you see, avarice doesn't need facts) who hit it big in penny stocks or garbanzo bean futures. People with prospector's mind-set believe these exaggerations without the slightest investigation, and think they can do it too. Scraping together a "grubstake," they go prospecting in the markets.

The compulsive behavior of prospectors' mentality bears a striking resemblance to an addiction. Once they're hooked, the addiction is hard to shake. Even poor results don't deter them. When one venture comes up dry, they just try another. They move to other mountains, but they never stop prospecting. They just keep promising themselves that they are different, entitled to wealth the easy way.

A MATTER OF TIME, NOT TIMING

"Hey, Joe, wanna hot tip? Buy 'em when they're low, and sell 'em when they're high." How can you argue with such logic? This tactic is called "timing the market" because you *time* your "buys" and your "sells" to correspond with the respective lows and highs of a given asset. Although the theory is clear and logical, the strategy is impossible to implement. When do we know that an asset is at its low point, and how do we know when it's hit its all-time high? It's not quite as simple as Will Rogers made it seem. "Take all your savings and buy some good stock and hold it till it goes up, then sell it. If it don't go up, don't buy it." Actually Will wasn't being serious; he was ribbing the same fallacy we're highlighting here.

Simply put, *you can't predict the unpredictable.* Everything from history to Nobel Prize-winning analysis attests that the timing approach is destined to fail. Despite all evidence to the contrary, some people persist in believing that *they* can outsmart the market, timing its highs and lows. It doesn't take long for them to stub their toes and fall face down on the turf. If they do it within their own portfolios, there's not much harm. They only hurt themselves. But, there are those who just will not keep their timing antics to themselves. They vainly try to lead followers to the pinnacles of success, feigning expertise in predicting which way the market will go. These "pinnacles" inevitably turn out to be unstable cliffs rather than solid summits. The whole scenario amounts to white-collar prospecting.

My advice? View the prospecting gurus and their high-priced advice with a healthy dose of caution. Nobody knows for sure where the markets are going. Educated opinions are worth consideration as we make our decisions, but never lose sight of the fact that nobody can predict the unpredictable. The forecasts and predictions are just educated guesses.

We can learn a lesson from history. As the 1980s began, the pundits were predicting skyrocketing inflation, steep interest rates, and runaway energy costs. There was virtual consensus on it. OPEC ruled the world, and no one would have dared suggest that inflation would suddenly drop back to earth. Marching inflation was as unshakeable as the Berlin Wall. Most savants were prophesying perilous times for Wall Street and the gold and silver advocates were predicting that the whole system would collapse.[1]

As events turned out, we could have made an opulent fortune by selling the experts short in the 1980s. OPEC lost its grip on the world's throat, inflation subsided, energy markets mimicked Humpty Dumpty, and interest rates (like the Berlin Wall) came tumbling down. Instead of trouble on Wall Street, the 1980s ushered in the strongest bull market in American history, and it forged upwardly for years.

Did I know all that was going to happen? No, and *neither did all the so-called gurus.* Take a look back at any Wall Street dive in the past—Black Monday, October 19, 1987; the market's decline in the fall of 1998; or the choppy gyrations of 2000. The experts on TV and radio were pounding our eardrums with forceful explanations of exactly *why* the market had done what it did, but not one of them could tell us with equal force and certainty to sell on the day before the market dropped. One can hardly argue with Paul Harwitz's quip: "We wouldn't be any worse off if we let the economists predict the weather and the meteorologists predict the economy."

If the facts on record were more widely known, most advisers and brokers make far more money from commissions than from brilliant moves in their own portfolios.[2] Would you think they'd spend all their time on the phone, dialing for dollars, if they were making money hand over fist in their own accounts? One of the best books on that subject was written by Fred Schwed (obviously a pen name). The title of his book says it all, *Where Are The Customers' Yachts?*[3]

Ask yourself why, if timing the market is so simple, people have to cheat, conniving for every morsel of insider information, in order to get rich on Wall Street. Without the illegal advantage of inside knowledge, at best, the timing game is just a crapshoot for the insiders too. Go to a library and check out all of the prophetic money books of the 1970s—the ones with the apocalyptic-sounding titles like *How to Prosper During the Coming Bad Years.* (That book depressed more people than the economy of the 1980s ever did.) Read the same type of books from the decades after, and you'll find yourself chuckling.[4]

With the clear advantage of perfect hindsight, we can easily see that the financial emperors have no clothes.

Market analysts and financial prognosticators do not have extrasensory powers. In fairness, most of them do not even claim such. It is we, in our greed, who wish they did. The very people who will look us in the eye and say, “There’s no such thing as free lunch,” will be the first ones to sue a brokerage if their advisers fail to perform. A personal integrity check is in order here.

And if we think the answer is to just go it alone, to play the market without expert advice and good research, we’re still missing the point. With or without good advisers, if we’re depending on timing rather than time, we’re still prospecting.

BUT WHAT ABOUT...

I was once challenged by a gentleman who said he was well acquainted with a man who had made tons of money in speculation. His friend had supposedly bought low and sold high in real estate, deal after deal, until he had arrived on Easy Street. I asked him, “Did your friend ever lose *any* money at all on real estate? Did every deal wind up making him money?” The honest answer was, “I don’t know.” I offered this thought, “Sure, we’ve all heard of people who’ve made a sweet deal or two, but the question is how well they have done overall. Net. What is the *total* picture?” (As an example, my father once tripled his money in a couple of months with a certain stock, but, if we take his total stock market experience, he’s wound up with only a thin margin of gain.) The man in my seminar said that he’d check it out and get back with me.

A few weeks later he called to report that we were *both right.* Since we seemed to be on opposite sides of table, I wasn’t sure how that could be. He said, up to a certain point his friend’s deals hadn’t gone anywhere but up. Each of four real estate transactions had made money. In fact, each deal had been a little better than the one before it because he had reinvested his profits from each preceding venture. At that point, he’d lost contact with his speculator friend. “I was right,” he emphasized, “he’d made a killing.”

“But,” he said, “now it’s your turn to be right.” His friend had rolled his profits into one more venture, leveraging a large apartment complex. Things had gone belly up and he’d lost it all. His speculator friend closed with a significant remark, “When it comes to investing, only your latest deal really counts."

The caller went on to say, "You see! You *can* get rich doing deals." I questioned him, as I wanted to see how he thought the foregoing was a success story. "Well, my friend was doing great until his last deal. I would have had the sense to quit while I was ahead. I wouldn't have done the last deal." Right! Classic prospectors' mentality.

PROSPECTING AND PROSPERITY

Two distinct mind-sets exist in the world of money. One leads to prosperity and peace of mind. The other leads to frustration, disappointment and a hunger that can't be satisfied.

Prospectors' Mentality: "I am the exception in the universe. The laws that apply to others do not apply to me."

Homesteaders' Mentality: "I am not an exception. I must apply the laws in order to receive the reward."

Prospector's mentality is very treacherous. The more we cater to it, the more powerful it grows. Those who don't rein it in may hit a vein of gold now and then, but they're unable to hang on to their gains. Riches don't satiate the hunger, they amplify it. The need for endless acquirement drives them to more speculation. They think they can do it one more time—this time bigger and better than ever before—and sooner or later they roll snake eyes and "crap out." Until they conquer the spirit of speculation, their financial future will always stand in jeopardy.

---

1. Howard J. Ruff, *How to Prosper During the Coming Bad Years,* Warner Books, New York, 1979.
2. C. David Chase, *Mugged on Wall Street,* Simon and Schuster, New York, 1987.
3. Fred Schwed, Jr., *Where Are the Customer's Yachts?* Fraser Publishing Co., Burlington, Vermont, 1940. You may be tempted to dismiss this book due to its age. That fact that the situation hasn't changed over the past decades *is the point!*
4. See the examples given in the next chapter.

CHAPTER 5

Fallacy No. 3: You Can't Get Rich on Safe Investments.

A common theme put forth in acquirement books is "If you're not risking a bundle, you're a moron." The authors seldom make their point that bluntly, but their implication is clear. They glorify risk and sneer at conservative measures. They herald the virtues of high risk investing so forcefully you'd think there was some direct and automatic connection between high risk and high return. There isn't one. And thinking that there is constitutes the biggest risk of all. Unless we're careful we can get swept up in their ideology, and lose our bearings (and shortly after that, our cash).

ALL WE HAVE TO FEAR...

Despite strong evidence to the contrary,[1] we still find a large percentage of the financial advisors and pundits advocating high risk investment tactics, contending that high risk is the main strategy used by the ultra-rich to become ultra-rich. "The first step toward successful investing is to determine your risk tolerance," goes the familiar refrain. Implicit in that statement is a minefield of explosively dangerous notions. It implies that risk is such a reliable tactic that the more we can stand the better, and that only our unfounded fears are holding us back. If we can bring ourselves to tolerate outrageous levels of risk, then let's cast off restraint, throw all caution to the wind and go for the gusto.

Once that type of thinking gets started, greed begins overriding wisdom, and a short trip to the pitfalls inevitably follows.

THE ONE-MINUTE MILLIONAIRE

If you've ever browsed the bookstores' personal finance sections, you may have marvelled at some of the titles on what could be called the "One-Minute Millionaire" shelf. You know the ones I mean—*How to Make a Fortune in Termite Futures, How to Profit From the Next Solar Eclipse, How to Start a Billion-Dollar Aerospace Business in Your Basement With Nothing Down.* They remind me of an ad that used to run in pulp magazines: "Draw this pirate and have an exciting career in neurosurgery," or something along those lines. These types of come-ons have grown a bit more sophisticated over time and also a bit longer. Some are book length.

Like mushrooms in a Bavarian forest, GRQ (Get-Rich-Quick) books—touting risk—sprout up beguiling people into thinking that the road to fabulous fortune is very fast and very easy. (We don't even have to draw the pirate anymore.)

Let me offer an example. The first sentence on the first page of a book on investment rules (yep, page one) reads, "Worry is not a sickness but a sign of health. If you are not worried, you are not risking enough."[2] Makes me sleep better already. How about you?

Another book that I've kept around—not because it's unique but because it's such a GRQ classic—is *The Omega Strategy* by William D. Montapert. Don't you love the eye-catching title? Sounds like an intrigue novel by Robert Ludlum. Anyway, the subtitle adds: "How You Can Retire Rich By The End Of The Eighties." Now that we're well past the eighties we can look back to see how useful and accurate the Omega Strategy would have been.

The book proclaims that the economy is going into a deflation cycle—short but pronounced. This contraction will be followed by a grand hyper-inflated surge with dire consequences for those who don't see it coming. Naturally, you and I have only one way to succeed—*The Omega Strategy.* It's our only hope.

The opening statement of the book declares:

> Once in a lifetime there comes a period of economic change so disruptive that those with very little money can seize the opportunity to become rich, while the very rich, seemingly protected by conservative investments, can be reduced to near poverty almost overnight. Such a time is now at hand. Here is the strategy.

Looking from today's perspective, there is only one thing to say, "oops."

If the author were here to defend his position, he'd probably say that his theory wasn't incorrect, just his timing. "It's sure to happen sometime soon in the 21st century. It just didn't happen when I originally thought it would." Personally, I have a hard time being impressed with someone who can predict ninety-nine of the next five catastrophes.

Permit me to extend this little foray a bit further. (We *are* having fun, aren't we?) On the back cover the publisher tells us what we are about to gain for our effort:

> Learn: why experts think speculating is the safest way to make money at this time. Why you and even the rich can't depend on cash, money market funds, Keogh and IRA plans, and other "safe" investments. How to pinpoint the end of the current deflation and make a killing when inflation zooms again...

Again, all of this was to transpire in the 1980s. Now, I am on the road quite a bit; the catastrophe must have happened while I was out of town. At least the book's title was accurate. Omega is the last letter in the Greek alphabet, and anyone who followed this strategy wound up in last place, too.

The GRQ advocates try to make us feel like financial wimps if we're not down in the market arenas, gladiating with the speculators. Extolling risk practically for its own sake, they tell us that "just getting into a car and driving to the grocery store is a risk." Philosophically, yes. Realistically, no. For the average, prudent person, the risk of driving to the store is so infinitesimally small that it's meaningless. (In the case of the grocery store, the risk comes after we get there.) Columnist Blackie Sherrod wasn't fooled. He quipped, "If you bet on a horse, that's gambling. If you bet you can make three spades, that's entertainment. If you bet cotton will go up three points, that's business. See the difference?"

Contrary to what the GRQ books imply, there is no automatic connection between the words "rich" and "risk." Furthermore, there are sound, prudent ways of investing that keep risk to a bare minimum, and these methods *do* have proven track records of success.[3]

THE ALL-IMPORTANT RETURN

Preserving principal is the first priority of sound investing. In a book that has withstood the test of time, *The Money Game* by Adam Smith, we find solid wisdom: "The first rule of making money is not to lose it!"[4]

Of course we want our principal to grow robustly, but we must maintain a healthy balance as we do so. Those who focus on the rate of return as their first priority are headed for trouble. Before long their glands start running their portfolio, and anyone who takes advice from his hormones will overpay for the education.

We've heard it many times: "If something's too good to be true, it usually is." More of us need to heed that warning. I distinctly recall an ad that ran prominently in my state. An organization calling itself "Investors Clearinghouse" promised guaranteed annual returns of 24 percent or greater. At the time I told my wife to make a mental note about ICH—we'd be hearing sad news in the future. That gut feeling proved to be correct. Within a year the news media were running stories about how Investors Clearinghouse had "cleared" hundreds of investors out of their nest eggs, and had "cleared" out of state. Tragically, many of the victims were retirees on fixed incomes. Some of these poor souls had taken their life's savings out of conservative vehicles, enticed by the glitter of phenomenal rates of return, and had paid dearly for their impatience.

Remember, remember: The return *of* your principal is more important than the return *on* your principal!

NOTES

1. Benjamin Graham, *The Intelligent Investor,* Fourth Revised Edition, Harper Business, New York, 1973.
Janet Lowe, *Warren Buffett Speaks: Wit and Wisdom from the World's Greatest Investor*, John Wiley & Sons, Inc., New York, 1997.
Thomas J. Stanley and William D. Danko, *The Millionaire Next Door: The Surprising Secrets of America's Wealthy*, Longstreet Press, Atlanta, GA., 1996.
Jane Bryant Quinn, "Rely on Buy-and-Hold Pattern for Stocks," *Business and Finance,* September 3, 1998, http://www.washingtonpost.com (September 27, 2000).
2. Max Gunther, *The Zurich Axioms,* New American Library, New York, page 1. Actually, parts of this book are very good, and I'd recommend it, were it not built on the premise that worry-inducing risk is the first axiom, and the one upon which all else is built.
3. Graham, Ibid.
Philip A. Fisher, *Common Stocks and Uncommon Profits,* John Wiley & Sons, Inc., New York, 1996.
Lowe, Ibid.
4. Adam Smith, *The Money Game,* First Edition Books, New York, 1976, p.3.

CHAPTER 6

Fallacy No. 4: Smart People Use OPM (Other People's Money)

About the only thing worse than losing a fortune is going to prison. Debt is prison—a metaphor that's been around for centuries, dating from a time when people who couldn't pay their debts were literally thrown into prison. Today, despite debt's detrimental effects on wealth and peace of mind, people still keep applying the manacles.

Clearly, one way we borrow ourselves into bondage is through the freewheeling abuse of credit. For decades personal bankruptcies have risen steadily,[1] climbing hand-in-hand with consumer debt and credit buying.[2] Regrettably, the trend shows no sign of abating.

"Credit card living" forms only part of the plague. Another facet involves consuming home equity in order to pay taxes, make home improvements, travel, and finance children's educations. Although these seem to be worthy purposes, in most cases they mask an underlying lack of discipline. For most of the twentieth century, people entered retirement with their homes paid for. That picture has shifted dramatically. More and more we see "retired" people still feeling the pressure of making house payments instead of putts on a golf course.

This eager willingness to mortgage the future to satisfy the desires of the present, and even pay interest on it, reflects lack of respect for the *time-value of money.* If we flout the interest equation—*paying* it instead of *receiving* it—we'll search in vain for financial health and freedom.

PRISON TERMS

Can you imagine walking into a bank and saying, "Hello, I want to borrow just enough money to get out of debt?" Some best-selling books have made assertions almost that outlandish. Especially popular is the ever-present version that advocates leveraging your way to wealth through investment in rental properties and "quick-fixer-upper" homes.

Here's an example:

> In fact, self-made wealth never comes without going into debt. I repeat: You can never become wealthy without going into some form of investment debt. And probably a lot of it...You can actually borrow your way to wealth.[3]

When some people read a paragraph like that they start breathing heavily, because they've borrowed before and they're good at it.

TIMELESS CAVEAT: BORROWER BEWARE

At least this author was straightforward about it. Most GRQ books avoid the word debt entirely (it is, after all, a four-letter word). Instead they use sophisticated sounding words like "leverage" or acronyms like OPM (Other People's Money).

Leverage makes speculators with acquirement mentality drool. To them it's a way of getting something for just about nothing. The aim is to gain control of an asset with as little money up front as possible. In exchange for that control, they agree to pay for the asset gradually over time or at some later date. The hope is that the asset will appreciate rapidly while they "own" it, so they can sell at a profit before the repayment and maintenance costs eat them alive. In short, leverage is an attempt to make a profit with timing and bravado.

One program (now thankfully defunct) actually utilized cheerleaders to work audiences into a frenzy, chanting "OPM! OPM!" as they waved pompoms. When we chant "OPM" out loud, it sounds a lot like "opium"—and it can be just as addictive.

In actuality, the real art in the whole scenario isn't the borrowing, it's the *selling!* Getting rid of the property—at a profit—is much easier said than done. The "asset" has to appreciate at a pretty good clip in order to cover the initial purchase price *plus* the interest *plus* the taxes, insurance, maintenance and repair costs. And that's not the end of it. You've got to add a few lawyer's fees (to evict the *&%#$ deadbeats who won't pay their rent) and also the advertising costs to run the rental ads, and then eventually, the cost to run your "For-Sale-Nothing-Down-Required" ad. If you're *that* good of a salesperson you don't need any of this to get rich. I'll gladly pay you handsome commissions to sell stuff I no longer want.

Those who advocate this strategy seldom give more than scant and feeble warnings about the myriad hazards one encounters. They glibly tell us to "buy low and sell high," offering not so much as an anemic paragraph on how to survive if the property should *decline* in value. Without solid people skills and sales savvy, incurring piles of debt (and a ton of maintenance nightmares) on run-down real estate is a recipe for disaster. Like acid, debt is a very caustic substance, and it needs to be handled with the same respect and care.

A CLASSIC EXAMPLE

The parameters for using OPM successfully are strict and limited. A lot of well-intentioned people have found that out. I've personally witnessed many tears rolling down the cheeks of those who got caught in the trap of "borrowing their way to wealth." The tactic does not even work for the gurus that promote it.

Albert Lowry, once called the "father of leveraged real estate," became the classic example, only not in the way he had hoped. Mr. Lowry authored *How You Can Become Financially Independent by Investing in Real Estate.* It was a best seller. His catchy hook line, "Give me only one hour a day and you can retire in three years," packed people into his programs. His income from the live presentations, books and tapes reached awe-inspiring levels and he was king of the road for a couple of years. But, life is a marathon, not a sprint, and his celebration of quick riches didn't go the distance. Some of his trusty little chunks of real estate became cement running shoes. He stumbled and fell face down on the track when one of his ventures near Lake Tahoe became a fiasco and a lesson in real estate reality. Lowry discovered that eventually OP want their M back—with I (Interest!)

One short decade after authoring his run-away best seller, he filed for bankruptcy. Not many of his students sent sympathy cards; they were mired in financial quagmires of their own.

The "leverage giants" do not and have not amassed the huge fortunes they imply. They may be able to cite a successful example or two but they never let us in on the whole picture—the net gain from all their leveraging contortions. One of Lowry's former partners became persona non grata as he set the record straight, testifying under oath, "I don't know any of them who made a fortune in real estate, either before they started teaching or since."

OPM + INTERNET + GREED = DAY TRADING

The vast possibilities of the internet to access information instantly, and the freedom and responsiveness of on-line brokerages are wonderful assets. With these tools prudent investors can gain company data, reports, analysis and near-inside information like never before. Knowledge about market and industry trends is also abundant. Couple that with a roaring bull market and we'd expect to see widespread success among stock investors. Unfortunately, such is not the case.

With easier access to OPM, and the continuing love affair with leverage, we are seeing the same old drama, played out with upgraded props. Studies show that the number of day traders—folks who trade in and out of volatile stocks, hoping to squeeze a profit out of jittering fluctuations in stock prices—grows annually, despite the documented fact that only about 10 percent of them ever turn a substantial or lasting profit,[4] amid the strongest bull market in U. S. history.

Here's how day traders attempt to use OPM and how they get into difficulty. Margin trading has been around for decades. Through this strategy, traders attempt to leverage their holdings and amplify profits by borrowing money from their brokerage firm. The brokerage lends the investor money based on the size of the investor's portfolio. Essentially the brokerage makes a loan, keeping the assets in the portfolio as collateral.

There are limits to the amount one can borrow. Let's say the margin limit is 50 percent.[5] If, then, we have $2000 in stock value in our portfolio, the brokerage would allow us to buy up to another $1000 in stocks.

So, let's say that we buy some stock for $100 per share on margin. In essence, we pay $50 and the brokerage puts up the other $50. If the stock rises to $150 and we sell, the brokerage gets its $50 back and we get the rest. We make $100 per share, doubling our money. Instead of making $50 profit on $100 invested (if we'd used only our own money), we'd have made $100 profit on $50 invested. You can see why, on paper, this strategy is so seductive.

Before you throw this book in the trash and go out and buy a bunch of GRQ books on day trading, I suggest you look at the flip side, and look at the real numbers about how well this strategy pays off in reality.

First, know this: If we buy a stock on margin and it drops, the brokerage will *politely* request that we pony up more cash to replace the "collateral" that was lost when the stock went down. This is what's known as a "margin call." And if we don't comply posthaste, the brokerage will *impolitely* liquidate our position and leave us with the empty cup (which comes in handy when we're shilling for hand-outs on the corner).

Keep in mind that the brokerage undertakes absolutely no risk when they lend us their money. They're set up to win either way. Either we add cash to always keep them in a 50 percent position or we have to liquidate before the stock value goes below what they've lent us. That's why they're happy to let us buy on margin. They make a little interest and another transaction fee with no risk. Neat, huh.

Now we get to the gruesome stuff. As tempting as margin trading may be, we need to keep in mind that the math works just as forcefully on the downside. Let's say that we bought the same stock for $100 per share on margin—$50 from us and $50 on loan from the brokerage. If instead of rising by 50 percent the stock drops by that much, it now sells for $50 per share instead of $100. We'd be "called" to put in more money[6] or liquidate. In this case we'd be asked to put up another $25 per share, so that brokerage maintains its 50-percent-of-value position. That would mean that we'd have paid $75 per share for a stock worth $50, and *still owe the brokerage $25 per share!*

Now we're really facing a dilemma. Do we pay the money with no guarantee that the stock won't just keep going south, devouring this "new money," and requiring more? And who knows how much more? Or, do we just bite the bullet and liquidate? Liquidating means the brokerage gets their $50 dollars back and we get exactly zero. Well not exactly zero. Modest though it might be, we'd owe the brokerage their transaction fee. (Just a little dash of salt for our open wound.)

In this case, leveraging doubled the loss. We have lost 100 percent when the stock dropped 50 percent. But, you say, let's cover the call, and hold on until the stock turns around. That's a possibility, *if* we've set aside a little cushion money to cover such contingencies. Because margin trading appeals to people with more avarice than caution, they seldom withhold even a dime to cover any setbacks. On the contrary, they're usually spread as thin as a razor, investing every cent and clawing for more, which is why they're so anxious to borrow the brokerage's money in the first place.

But just to see where that strategy would put us, let's say that we manage to scrape together the $25 per share required to cover the first call. If the stock turned around right at that point and went back up, then we would've dodged the bullet and would only be out a few valium. But what if it doesn't turn around at that point? Let's just say that it muddles for the next couple of years. We've tied up a wad of cash and our stomach lining, receiving no compensation for our pains.

Worse yet, let's say that it drops another 10 or 20 percent. Now we're so far under water the fish have headlights, because we'd be cordially invited to add even more cash on the merciless margin call that would ensue, and we've further compounded our misery. We suffer *twice the loss* for every percent the stock tanks, and have to tie up even more money for the privilege. And then what if it muddles? Now we're sitting on an agonizing loss for who knows how long, yearning every day for the stock to turn around.

Bear in mind that the brokerage can't lose, but for the margin trader there's no such protection. In volatile markets they can be wiped out in a matter of hours.

HEY, WE'RE ALL ADULTS HERE

Perhaps you read about the pathetic lawsuit filed against an online discount brokerage by the 27-year old grad student who experienced the abrupt bursting of his leverage bubble. "It all happened within three days," he whined. "The market took a huge dive, the valuation of my stocks went to roughly half...that's when [the brokerage] decided to sell my stocks."

Entranced by a few early gains in the market, the man learned about margin trading and dove off the high board. When his stocks tanked, and he didn't meet his margin calls in a timely manner, the brokerage wasted no time in covering its interest. The next sound the "investor" heard was *flush.*

"I was never informed of the risk. I was never told that on a margin account they could sell all of this. And it would have been nice to know that had they seen I was investing or overextending to the limit on my margin credit, they would have [told] me." (I'll bet this guy gets real upset with traffic cops when they see him not wearing his seat belt, and they don't come up and spank him.)

By the way, the stocks he leveraged weren't dogs, either. He'd picked some of the market darlings of the season. The point is that even the good stuff has enough erratic ups and downs to do you in when you're leveraged.

THAT AIN'T ALL FOLKS

Additionally, costs are woven into this strategy that are not only sobering but they also help to explain why, in the final analysis, most day traders lose. First, even at discount rates, commissions soar. Most on-line discount brokerages charge a modest $7 to $12 per transaction. Most day traders average 10 to 12 trades each day, resulting in costs of $350-$700 per week. Second, day traders forfeit long-term capital gains advantages on their taxes. Every one of their victories is taxed as a short-term gain, and they pay (at current rates) 15 percent or higher directly to Uncle Sam. Third, although the rates are relatively conservative, the investor does pay the brokerage interest on the borrowed money.

Overall, the major reason day traders cannot achieve substantial and lasting profits has already been covered: *You can't predict the unpredictable.* No amount of pseudo-scientific chart reading, trend analysis, momentum monitoring, or tea-leaf reading can overcome the fact that the market is so capricious and volatile that no one knows for sure, from one minute to the next, which way it's going to go. Day traders, in the end, are just flipping coins.

Studies, utilizing exceptionally large samples, show that the day traders have gone in the wrong direction. Rather than taking the micro-view, zeroing in on momentary blips on the daily screen, the successful odds lie with the macro-view. A broad-spectrum approach over a long term has repeatedly been shown to be the best way to buffer market gyrations and make money, consistently, in stocks.[7]

CONSEQUENCES ON A BIGGER SCALE

Just so you don't run out of things to worry about, there's a bigger implication with the rampant abuse of OPM. Federal Reserve figures show that margin debt has burgeoned along with the great bull market. In fact, margin debt has actually grown at triple the rate of household consumer debt (which we've already mentioned is no small issue). "So what?" you say.

Here's the concern: A growing portion of the "value" in the stock market is a self-feeding illusion—a house of cards that could come crashing down one day. Stock value is driven by the law of supply and demand as we all know. As more people buy stocks prices increase, building "value" in portfolios. That allows investors to buy more stocks on margin which drives up the price of stocks building even more "collateral" in the portfolio, thereby feeding the cycle one more time.

But what happens when the upward momentum stalls? (Notice I said when, not if.) In the absence of this somewhat self-perpetuating propulsion, values will begin to come down. That will cause a reduction in "collateral," spawning margin calls. On a limited basis there's little reason for concern, but once values start declining, the momentum could build until it reached critical mass resulting in a dramatic implosion.

We got a little taste of this in the spring of 2000, when there was a sharp sell-off in technology stocks. Suddenly, values dropped and margin calls began popping up like acne on a teenager. The cascading effect was evident but didn't reach critical mass, and the market stabilized. Even on that scale many portfolios suffered severe "collateral" damage and some others were wiped out entirely.[8]

I hope this won't keep you up tonight. It probably won't happen until 2029.[9]

COUNT ALL THE COSTS

As we sum up, let me make one thing clear: I am not disparaging real estate or stocks as investment vehicles. I'm sounding the warning about ill-considered mind-sets and imprudent *ways of investing* in those vehicles. The caution being raised is about the most dangerous element in any investment or business scenario—a flippant attitude toward debt.

Whenever you enter into any investment, count the costs—not just the hard dollar costs—but *all* the costs. Investors pay fees in more ways than dollars. How much time, effort and attention (mind power!) will be invested before you're through? How much tending and managing will the investment require? Weigh those expenses carefully. And make sure you notice how much heavier the weight becomes if you are leveraged or are using borrowed money. Debt has a way of prowling through our thoughts, gnawing at our peace of mind—a mental distraction of the first order. In the long run, time and mental freedom are currencies with higher value than money.

---

1. Robert M. Lawless, "The Relationship Between Nonbusiness Bankruptcy Filings and Various Basic Measures of Consumer Debt, *Relationship of US Bankruptcy Filings and Consumer Debt,* October 4, 2000, http://law.missouri.edu/lawless_bkr/body_Index.htm (October 13, 2000).
2. Fitch Ratings BusinessWire, *"Credit Card ABS Issuance Surges Despite Warning Sign,"* September 28,2000, http://finance.individual.com/display_news.asp?doc (October 2, 2000).
3. Robert G. Allen, *Creating Wealth,* Simon and Schuster, New York, 1983, p.16. Undoubtedly there is an egregious typo in the title. It should have been "Creating Welts".
4. Jeff Fisher, *"The Perils of Day Trading,"* February 11, 1999, http://www.intellectualcapital.com/issues/issue39item631.asp (September 1, 2000).
"Report of the Day Trading Project Group: Findings and Recommendations," *NASAA Project Group on Day Trading,* August 9, 1999, http://www.nasa.org/daytradingreport.htm (September 1, 2000).
"State Securities Regulators Highlight Problems with Day Trading," NASAA, August 9, 1999, http://wwwnasa.org/whoweare/media/dtreportrelease.htm (September 1, 2000).
5. Fifty percent is the current legal limit. See Regulation T.
6. The brokerage never accepts an iota of risk. When the value drops, the investor must immediately pay sufficient cash to the brokerage to maintain its 50 percent position relative to the value of the stock. Brokerages waste no time in protecting themselves.

NOTES

7. John C. Bogle, *Bogle on Mutual Funds,* Irwin Professional Publishing, Burr Ridge, Illinoise, 1994, pp. 4-13.
8. World-Current Events-2000 Month-By-Month, *National News,* April 2000, http://wwwinfoplease.com/ipa/A0801103.html (October 19, 2000).
Jane Bryant Quinn, "Rely on Buy-and-Hold Pattern for Stocks," *Business and Finance,* September 3, 1998, http://www.washingtonpost.com (September 27, 2000).
9. Though there have been laws and regulations put in place to prevent another meltdown, it was the landslide of margin calls that triggered the crash of 1929.

CHAPTER 7

Fallacy No 5: Times Are Different Now

Virtually every book on the "One-Minute Millionaire" shelf starts with wording to the effect that time-proven principles are no longer valid—*times are different now.* The only thing that varies is the amount of alarm the authors choose to inject into their pitch. (Although this line is often the *opener* for the latest financial fad, I've saved it for last because it leads into a needed discussion on principles and parameters.) Some authors are moderately subdued, while others attempt to work the reader into fevered hysteria. Some would have us believe that the world is already on the brink of an economic apocalypse that'll destroy governments and all social order.

The level of alarm may vary, but the essence is this: "Never before in the entire history of civilization have we encountered the unprecedented combination of economic factors now before us. This unique set of circumstances makes all previous wisdom outdated and obsolete. The sound principles and practices of the past, though they may have worked well for centuries, will no longer work." They must be rejected and replaced with the revolutionarily *new* and astute techniques of the same person sounding the alarm. That's been the leading line in the oldest cons in the world. Whenever you hear—"Once in a lifetime opportunity! Act fast!" my advice is "CAVEAT LECTOR" (Latin for, "Run, man, RUN!)[1]

CATCH YOUR BREATH

Before we go stampeding with the lemmings in pursuit of the latest investment gimmick let's slow down, breathe through our nose, and take a good look at some time-proven wisdom. Success, wealth and fulfillment (none of which are necessarily synonymous) are achieved and maintained by compliance with the principles and laws that yield them. In the universe, every effect has a cause, and we reap what we sow.[2]

Correct principles don't come and go with the tides. They are neither circumstantial nor contingent. No less than the most successful investor of our times, Warren Buffett, declared, "If principles can become dated, they're not principles."[3] That's the central difference between a principle and a technique. A principle is unaffected by transient conditions, holding enduring rather than conditional value. It's precisely that quality *that* constitutes their worth. Even when we're confronted with unexpected situations, a principle will point to a pathway that brings clarity to the confusion.

Bottom line: Ignore the hype and glitzy promotions. Don't be swayed by current popularity or sexy advertising. Opt instead for the tried-and-proven methods of sound money management that have withstood the acid test—the test of time. When you encounter an intriguing investment strategy, don't get in a hurry. Investigate it thoroughly. Analyze it from the "standpoint of principles." Are the underlying premises of this particular technique based on long-standing principles with proven validity? Does the technique benefit all parties? Or, is it a "hit-and-run," "something-for-nothing," "who-cares-how-it-works-it-just-does" kind of stratagem?

TIMELY AND TIMELESS

In reality, the economic conditions that exist today are not totally without precedent. Times *are not* all that different now. Facades change, but the essences do not. Adopting a financial game plan that will prove effective in virtually any climate is possible; and such a strategy is based on principles that won't disappoint. Study any truly successful businessperson or investor and you'll see the recurrent pattern. The basic principles keep showing up. They're not glamorous, but they've withstood all the tests.

Take, for example, the financial recommendations made by one of the icons of U.S. history, Ben Franklin. The legacy of wisdom (and wit) handed down through *Poor Richard's Almanac* and his other essays on money management is classic. First, note Franklin's forthright admission that these principles were even "old fashioned" in his day: "Not a tenth part of the wisdom he ascribed to me was my own, but rather the gleanings I had made of the sense of all ages and nations."[4] His prosperity principles were well known (but, like today, not necessarily well practiced) even in the 1700s! How meaningful is that?

Franklin's advice was not complex; and it still works today. He taught these principles:

1. Work Hard
2. Live Providently
3. Avoid Debt
4. Harness Compounding

Testimonial to the fact that these principles hold true in modern times, a study of the methods employed by Warren Buffett shows that these same core principles resonate with him, his business partners, and *his* mentors. We'll examine Buffett's methods of investing later. For now, take my word for it, Buffett's methods bear a striking resemblance to Ben Franklin's. The only difference is the phrasing. Instead of saying, "Harness Compounding," Buffett would say "Harness Growth."

BEN'S MAP

Here's a sampling of Ben Franklin's wisdom:

1. WORK HARD

"The taxes are indeed very heavy, and if those laid on by the government were the only ones we had to pay, we might more easily discharge them; but we have many others, and much more grievous to some of us. We are taxed twice as much by our idleness..."[5]

"God helps them that help themselves."[6]

"Sloth, like rust, consumes faster than labor wears. The used key is always bright."[7]

"The sleeping fox catches no poultry."[8]

"Sloth makes all things difficult, but industry all easy. Laziness travels so slowly that poverty soon overtakes him."[9]

"Then plough deep while sluggards sleep, and you shall have corn to sell and keep."[10]

2. LIVE PROVIDENTLY

"A man may, if he knows not how to save as he gets, keep his nose all his life to the grindstone, and die not worth a groat at last."[11] (He blows too much money on reconstructive nose surgery.)

"Tis easier to suppress the first desire than to satisfy all that follow it."[12]

"Pride breakfasted with plenty, dined with poverty, and supped with infamy."[13]

"Beware of little expenses; a small leak will sink a great ship."[14]

"At a great pennyworth pause a while, many have been ruined by buying good pennyworths."[15]

3. AVOID DEBT

"He that goes a borrowing goes a sorrowing."[16]

"But what madness must it be to run in debt for these superfluities (Fancy clothing, dainty cakes, etc.).... But, ah, think what you do when you run in debt; you give to another power over your liberty!"[17]

"Those have a short Lent, who owe money to be paid at Easter."[18]

"Rather go to bed supperless than rise in debt."[19]

4. HARNESS COMPOUNDING

"Remember that Money is of a prolific generating Nature. Money can beget Money, and its Offspring can beget more, and so on. He that kills a breeding Sow, destroys all her offspring to the thousandth Generation. He that murders a Crown, destroys all it might have produced even Scores of Pounds."[20]

Franklin not only taught the power of thrift, he lived the principle of compounding. As an example, he bestowed on the cities of Boston and Philadelphia an endowment of 1000 pounds each. The endowments were to go untouched for 100 years. Through the power of compounding, a large sum would result which would benefit the cities in perpetuity.

Two centuries after the initial gift, Boston and Philadelphia still enjoy the benefits of Franklin's industry, thrift, and wise use of interest. Everything from city development (and redevelopment) to scholarships for medical students have been financed by this wisdom.

FROM FOUNDATION UPWARD

The principles just mentioned aren't the only ones we'll employ to achieve financial strength, but they're at the core of a comprehensive Wealth Plan that will be described in detail. The key decision to make at this point is to cease the courtship of Lady Luck and to make a full commitment to sound principles. To profess belief in the law of the harvest while continuing to prospect for quick, easy riches is more than a mild contradiction. If you really believe in the law of the harvest, then stop prospecting and focus on plowing, planting, and cultivating!

---

1. Actually the correct translation is "let the reader beware."
2. Jeffrey Moses, *Oneness: Great Principles Shared by All Religions,* Ballantine Books, New York, 1989, p.39-41.
3. Janet Lowe, *Warren Buffett Speaks: Wit and Wisdom from the World's Greatest Investor,* John Wiley & Sons, Inc., New York, 1997. p.86.
4. Benjamin Franklin, *The Way to Wealth,* originally published in 1758. Reprinted in: Peter Shaw, *The Autobiography and Other Writings by Benjamin Franklin,* Bantam Books, New York, 1982, page 193.
5. Ibid., p. 186.
6. Benjamin Franklin, Poor Richard's Almanac, June, 1736.

NOTES

7. Benjamin Franklin, The Way to Wealth, originally published in 1758. Reprinted in: Peter Shaw, The Autobiography and Other Writings by Benjamin Franklin, Bantam Books, New York, 1982, page 186.
8. Ibid.
9. Ibid.
10. Ibid.
11. Ibid., p. 188.
12. Ibid., p. 190.
13. Ibid., p. 191.
14. Ibid., p. 189.
15. Ibid.
16. Ibid., p. 190.
17. Ibid., p. 191.
18. Ibid., p. 192.
19. Ibid.
20. Benjamin Franklin, Advice to a Young Tradesman, 1748.

Section III

THE PARAMETERS

CHAPTER 8

Getting Beyond Paycheck-To-Paycheck Living

The first milestone on the road to financial freedom is to get beyond "paycheck-to-paycheck living." Those who don't have ready explanations: "My employer isn't paying me what I'm worth," or "My boss won't give me a raise," or "Things cost too much these days," or "My spouse doesn't make as much as he [or she] should," or "The government doesn't do enough." The list goes on, but you get the idea.

None of those answers gets to the truth. After all the excuses are listed, the fact remains that people live paycheck to paycheck because they live paycheck to paycheck. Before you say, "Well, duh Deaton, that's brilliant," hear me out. Spending our entire paycheck is not due to demonic external forces, the alignment of the planets, or defective chips in our hard drives. It's a lack of discipline. If you're frequently short of cash before your next paycheck arrives, you had better wake up. The problem is *you!*

It may be true that a few of us need to ply our skills more diligently to increase our value to the marketplace and expand our income, but in most cases it's not about the size of the paycheck. Paycheck-to-Paycheck Syndrome results from a lack of discipline, not lack of income.

THE SPANISH IMPOSITION

In mid-October, people in the United States acknowledge the arrival of Christopher Columbus to the continents now called the Americas. Referring to the "new" lands as the Indies, Columbus claimed them for the Spanish monarchy. Over the ensuing decades, the Spaniards diligently ransacked these continents. They gathered up fortunes of gold, silver, turquoise and precious spices, and shipped it all back to Spain by the boatloads. Yet, history plainly records that the Spanish monarchy went bankrupt. Benjamin Franklin's quip serves as an apt reminder still today: "The Indies did not make Spain rich because her outgoes were greater than her incomes."[1] (The gain in Spain went mainly down the drain.)

Ultimately there's only one valid answer to the question, "Why am I stuck in paycheck-to-paycheck living?" "I haven't made an all-out commitment to the laws of accumulation." Unless and until we make that inner change, nothing will ever substantially alter in our monetary life, no matter how much money we make.

THE RICHEST MAN IN BABYLON

Here's a timeless solution for paycheck-to-paycheck living: In 1926 George S. Clason, a financial writer for eastern newspapers, wrote a series of "Babylonian Parables" dealing with personal financial management. The articles were collected and published as a book under the title of the best-known of these short allegories. That book, *The Richest Man in Babylon,* has since become a financial classic.[2] I strongly endorse its concepts and recommend you read it at least once a year and teach it to your offspring.

Schooled by a wealthy elder, a young man named Arkad progresses from a hand-to-mouth existence to become the richest man in his country, Babylon. Arkad's big breakthrough comes when his mentor emphasizes that he must grasp that *a part of all he earns is his to keep.* Arkad does not immediately grasp the point, and declares that *all* he earns is his to keep. Patiently, his teacher points out that he must pay others to make his way through life. A portion of his earnings goes to others in compensation for the goods and services he receives from them. But if all his earnings pass through his fingers, he'll wind up as little more than a slave, working for his food and clothing.

The wise elder impresses on Arkad that he must learn *to pay himself first.* Before he disburses a single penny from his earnings, he must set aside a portion of his income—10 percent—so he can make some of his money work for him. The light clicks on in Arkad's mind and he makes the commitment to pay himself first. Living on 90 percent of his income, he soon finds that his lifestyle doesn't diminish much and that he's able to build a "workforce" to provide a comfortable future. Month by month his savings grow and so does his commitment to keep the momentum going by living within his income.

HOW IT'S DONE

The lessons Arkad learned will pay huge dividends for all of us. We must:

1. Live on less than we earn.
2. Pay ourself first.

These two rules work as an inseparable team to cure paycheck-to-paycheck syndrome. The best way to live rule number one is to live rule number two. Pay yourself first! Every month. No matter what. Decide on a certain fixed percentage, and do it. Set that percentage aside *before* you do anything else. Live on the remainder. If we expect the savings to show up *after* we are done spending, it'll never happen.

Choose a realistic percentage, yet one that will stretch you a little bit. Saving that percentage each month may not at first be easy, but once you get it going it does become easier. Ralph Waldo Emerson said: "That which we persist in doing becomes easier; not that the nature of the thing has changed, but our ability to do it has increased."

By exercising the first two rules from *The Richest Man In Babylon* we develop discipline and mental muscle, which is a paycheck all its own—a paycheck that only we can give to ourselves.

COMPOUNDING SUCCESS

There remains one other key principle to glean from *The Richest Man In Babylon.* Twelve months after the first lesson, the wealthy elder, Algamish, returns to check on his pupil. "What progress have you made since I last saw you?" he asks. "I have paid myself faithfully," Arkad replies, explaining that he has put his money to work earning interest. Algamish commends Arkad, "That is good. And what do you do with the rental (interest)?" Arkad replies, "I do have a great feast with honey and fine wine and spiced cake. Also I have bought myself a scarlet tunic. And someday I shall buy a Corvette!" (oops, sorry.) "...a young ass on which to ride." To which Algamish laughs and says, "You do eat the children of your savings!"

Algamish then shares the third rule of prosperity. He tells Arkad that he must learn to multiply his workforce—each gold piece that he saves is a worker, who can not only work for him but who can recruit other workers, who can also work for him. All those workers can recruit yet another—even larger—batch of workers, and so on. Summing up, Algamish declares, "First get thee an army of golden [workers], then many a rich banquet will you enjoy without regret!"

Rule number three from *The Richest Man In Babylon:*

3. Let your savings compound.

Part of what we earn—ten percent (or whatever we've chosen)—must be put to work both earning and "recruiting" other earners. Interest accrued on the ten percent is not spent (until we've reached our freedom goal) but is added to the workforce to amplify the earning power of our savings. Those dollars remain in the fray, earning and recruiting, month after month as well. *This is the principle of compounding.*

---

1. Benjamin Franklin, *The Way to Wealth,* originally published in 1758. Reprinted in: Peter Shaw, *The Autobiography and Other Writings by Benjamin Franklin,* Bantam Books, New York, 1982, page 189.
2. George S. Clason, *The Richest Man in Babylon,* Hawthorn/Dutton, New York, 1926-1955.

CHAPTER 9

The Power of Compounding

One of the lovable characters from American literature is Mark Twain's articulate knave, Tom Sawyer. Well known is the episode when Tom has been assigned by his Aunt Polly to paint the fence, a task he does not relish. Indignant, he unenthusiastically begins to paint by himself. Before long, however, Tom's keen mind hatches a plan to liberate himself from the hands-on drudgery. By conveying that whitewashing a fence is some sort of diversion, he finds a way to enlist the help of others. Within minutes, several of Tom's friends are "enjoying" all the fun of completing Tom's task for him. Young Mr. Sawyer winds up in a hands-free supervisory role. (Mark Twain ought to be credited with having written the first American management text.)

Two lessons can be learned from Tom Sawyer's methods. First, what constitutes "work" and what constitutes "play" is a matter of perspective. One person's work is another person's recreation. But the second lesson is more applicable to our current topic. Basically there are two ways of getting a job done—do it ourself or harness the power of a team. When it comes to accruing a living income, each of us can be the sole earner or we can harness the power of a portion of our respective earnings. (A third choice exists, I suppose, but charity and welfare are untenable for most of us.) Ultimately, if we live long enough, not even the first choice will be an option. If we don't learn how to put money to work for us, we'll face grim repercussions in our old age.

THE IMPACT OF TIME

Compound interest is the greatest wealth-building principle on the planet. Two crucial factors determine precisely how much power we derive from it—the amount of time we harness, and the annual percentage rate (interest rate).[1] The following examples will illustrate the impact of time.

PETER MINUIT BUYS MANHATTAN

Colloquial history recounts that Peter Minuit, of the Dutch West India Company, made a shrewd land deal a few centuries back. In 1626, Minuit supposedly "purchased" the entire island of Manhattan for $24 worth of costume jewelry. (As it turned out, the Native Americans who actually received the jewelry weren't even the tribe who held possession of the island. So, you can decide for yourself who duped whom.) "What a deal!" we exclaim. At first glance it would seem so. The land Minuit obtained—the primest of prime, "beach front" property—now values in the range of $30-40 billion. Land value has grown impressively, but "the rest of the story" is equally impressive. Observe the growth of the Minuit family fortune if Peter had banked that $24 and the family had averaged a modest six percent return, compounded annually:

YEAR	ACCOUNT VALUE
1626	$24
1726	$8,143
1826	$2,763,022
1926	$937.499,017
2000	$70,000,000,000
2026	$300,000,000,000

Rather than owning a parcel of land worth $35 billion, which they would have had to maintain and manage, the Minuits would now have over twice that much. By the 400th anniversary of the "great land deal," in the year 2026, the Minuit bank account would stand at over $300 billion. Pretty impressive.

A TALE OF TWO INVESTORS

Two investors, A and B, each earn ten percent on their money, and each saves $2,000 per year. Investor A, however, starts early. Beginning at age 25, she deposits $2,000 per year for eight years and then stops. She puts in a total of $16,000. Investor B procrastinates for those 8 years, and then gets going. She puts in $2,000 each year for the succeeding 28 years. She invests a total of $56,000. Now here's the thunderbolt—Investor B is still playing catch up! At age 60, Investor A enjoys a total of $345,817, and Investor B has $239,262 in her account. Morale of the story: *Start early*—harness as much time as you can. If you haven't started already, *start now!*

INVESTOR A			INVESTOR B		
Age	Tax-Deferred Contribution	Year-End Value	Age	Tax-Deferred Contribution	Year-End Value
25	$2,000	$2,200	25	$0	$0
26	$2,000	$4,620	26	$0	$0
27	$2,000	$7,282	27	$0	$0
28	$2,000	$10,210	28	$0	$0
29	$2,000	$13,431	29	$0	$0
30	$2,000	$16,974	30	$0	$0
31	$2,000	$20,872	31	$0	$0
32	$2,000	$25,159	32	$0	$0
33	$0	$27,675	33	$2,000	$2,200
34	$0	$30,442	34	$2,000	$4,620
35	$0	$33,487	35	$2,000	$7,282
36	$0	$36,835	36	$2,000	$10,210
37	$0	$40,519	37	$2,000	$13,431
•	•	•	•	•	•
•	•	•	•	•	•
56	$0	$247,809	56	$2,000	$194,694
57	$0	$272,590	57	$2,000	$216,364
58	$0	$299,849	58	$2,000	$240,200
59	$0	$329,834	59	$2,000	$266,240
60	$0	$362,817	60	$2,000	$295,262
Less Total Invested		**(16,000)**	**Less Total Invested**		**(56,000)**
Net Earnings		**$ 345,817**	**Net Earnings**		**$ 239,262**

THE RULE OF 72

Have you seen the handy little rule for calculating interest growth in your head? It's called the "Rule of 72," and it's a simple way to determine the length time required to double any given principal. Simply divide the number 72 by the interest rate. The result equals the number of years required to double our money. If, for example, we're earning eight percent on our money, it'll take nine years to double it ($72 \div 8 = 9$). If we're earning 10 percent on our money, it'll take a little over seven years (7.2) to double our original amount ($72 \div 10 = 7.2$).

ACCUMULATING A MILLION

Here's another way to visualize the impact of time on compounding: What does it take to save a million dollars; that is, how much money would we have to put aside per month if our goal were to save one million dollars? The answer depends on how much help we want from time and the power of compounding.

Let's suppose that we earn nine percent compounded monthly on our money, and we're in a hurry to own our million dollars. Here's what we'd be looking at.

YEARS	TOTAL PYMTS	MONTHLY AMT
5	60	$13,258

If we wanted to save $1 million in five years we'd have to save over $13,250 *per month* for the sixty-month period! Now that's quite a lot. Not many could do that. But let's harness the power of time, consistency and patience and see what happens.

YEARS	TOTAL PYMTS	MONTHLY AMT
10	120	$5,167
20	240	$1,497

By doubling the time frame, we reduce the monthly amount substantially—by much more than half! Why? Because our earnings are earning. Our first generation of workers recruited a second generation. And, working together, those two generations recruited a third generation, at an even faster rate. And so on.

Each generation becomes larger and more powerful. We're enjoying the benefits of the "snowballing" effect. Our quest begins modestly but, with the passing of time, the momentum builds and the results become robust.

The twenty-year goal comes within the reach of many, but if the monthly amount is still too steep, we just add more time.

YEARS	TOTAL PYMTS	MONTHLY AMT
25	300	$891
30	360	$546
35	420	$337
40	480	$211
45	540	$134

This illustration shows the impact of time on our monetary goals. Those who start early are rewarded. Their ascent can be gradual, reasonable and attainable. On the other hand, the grade becomes steep for those who procrastinate.

ANOTHER VIEW

Using the same parameters described above, let's see how much of our own money is involved at the various plateaus. In each case we'll end up with $1 million, but the contributions will differ markedly:

YEARS	MONTHLY AMT	TOTAL DEPOSIT
5	$13,258	$795,501

In this case, we've achieved our $1 million, but we've had to do most of the work ourself. Only about 20 percent of our goal was contributed by interest.

If, however, we have patience and can harness more time, look at the difference:

GOAL: ACCUMULATE $1,000,000

YEARS	MONTHLY AMT	TOTAL DEPOSIT
10	$5,167	$620,109
20	$1,497	$359,356
25	$891	$267,558

YEARS	MONTHLY AMT	TOTAL DEPOSIT
30	$546	$196,642
35	$337	$141,661
40	$211	$101,750
45	$134	$72,376

The combined power of time and compound interest comes through loud and clear. In the case of the 30-year program, interest contributed 80 percent of the goal.

In summary, the goal of being a millionaire is within the reach of virtually anyone who *really wants* it. Save $900 per month at nine percent (compounded monthly) for twenty-five years, for example, and you'll be a millionaire.

THE ESSENTIAL LESSONS

Two points are clear. One: The longer we employ the power of compounding the more dramatic and positive its effect. Two: Procrastination is a deadly enemy.

---

1. John C. Bogle, *Bogle on Mutual Funds,* Irwin Professional Publishing, Burr Ridge, Illinois, 1994, pp. 3-13.

CHAPTER 10

Calibrating the Course

No one stumbles onto financial freedom. The course is a strategically-designed journey with a specific destination in mind and a well-thought-out plan for achieving it. Before we move to defining the destination and designing the plan, we need to carefully consider a major feature of the territory ahead—inflation.

A WORD ON INFLATION

A rose may be a rose, but a dollar is not so constant. The dollar today does not buy what it did even one decade ago. For example, from 1956 to 1986 (a period with both high and low inflationary episodes), the dollar lost 74 percent of its buying power. In other words, a dollar in 1956 would buy *four times* what it could in 1986. From 1980 to 2000, a period of moderate to low inflation, the dollar still lost over half of its value. It took $207.77 in 2000 to buy what $100 would buy in 1980.[1]

If the value of the dollar *diminishes,* why do they call it *inflation?* The answer has to do with the law of supply and demand. The value of the dollar deflates whenever the number of dollars inflates disproportionately. When the government prints and puts into circulation more money than warranted by the rise in goods and services, the value of the dollar falls. Inflated numbers mean deflated value.

Inflation isn't new. It's been around for centuries—ever since man began exchanging currency for some type of commodity or service. Inflation is not necessarily bad either. Almost all economists agree that a mild amount of inflation is actually healthy. The key issue is the *rate* at which the inflation's occurring. In the United States, during the 1950s and early 1960s, inflation averaged about two percent per year. In the '90s it averaged 2.8 percent.[2] During these times, the dollar lost value, but the rate was low and the impact on purchasing power was gradual.

In the '50s no one ever talked about inflation, but in the 1970s it became a household word as inflation rose to 11 percent in 1974, averaged close to nine percent per year for the rest of the decade, and topped out at 13.5 percent in 1980.[3] The *rate* of inflation had accelerated to the point that people could actually feel the effects. The dollar was shrinking, and they felt it at the grocery store, at the automobile dealership—everywhere. Clerks would rush up and raise the price of something on the shelf, right in front of shoppers who were making up their minds to buy it. And if they did decide to buy it, and didn't *sprint* to the checkout stand, the price would go up a couple of times on their way to pay for it—or so it seemed.

This awakening had its good points (even if the high inflation didn't). People realized that they couldn't retire at today's values and be comfortable, they had to give more forethought to future values.

The ones who got hit hardest were the people who had retired in the '40s, '50s and '60s. Many thought they'd planned for an adequate retirement, but by the end of the '70s they found themselves underfunded. Their income was fixed, but their purchasing power was not. They fell further behind with each passing day. The government made attempts to soften the blow with "cost-of-living" adjustments to the social security allotments. Despite those adjustments, many of our elderly wound up in tough straits.

Fortunately, we don't need to learn this lesson the hard way. We've been forewarned, and we'd better use that knowledge. Inflation hasn't vanished, and we need to make our plans and projections for the future with that in mind.

THE "HALF-LIFE" OF MONEY

As we look to the future, visualizing the "half-life" of money is imperative. Here's what I mean: As inflation creeps along, eroding the value of the dollar each year, after a certain number of years, a dollar would buy only half of what it does today. The number of years it takes for money to lose half its value is its "half-life." Obviously, the higher the rate of inflation, the faster this happens.

A quick way of calculating this effect is to use the Rule of 72 once again. Simply, divide the rate of inflation into 72 and that'll tell us the half-life or the number of years it would take for money to lose half its value. For example, if inflation were averaging 6 percent per year, the half-life of money would be 12 years (72 ÷ 6 = 12). In other words, every 12 years the purchasing power of the dollar would be cut in half, or the cost of living would double, however we wanted to look at it.

ILLUSTRATING THE POINT

Applying this thinking to a real-world example, we can see the dramatic significance. Let's assume that a 25-year old man wants to retire at age 61 on the equivalent annual income of $50,000 in today's terms and that he can average 10 percent per year on his investments. Doing his math, he calculates the size of his needed retirement nest egg as follows:

$$\frac{\$50{,}000}{10\%} = \$500{,}000$$

A lump sum of $500,000, making 10 percent per year, would yield $50,000 per year or a little over $4100 per month. This looks comfortable to him right now, but if he doesn't take inflation into account he'll wind up destitute. Here's why.

If we assume an inflation rate of four percent,4 the half-life of money would be 18 years (72 x 4 = 18). That means that money will lose half its value every 18 years. Since there are two 18-year intervals between ages 25 and 61, it means that his purchasing power will be cut in half twice before he even gets to his goal. Eighteen years from now, when the man is forty-three, $4100 would purchase only half of what it did when he started out. In other words, he'd have to get by on the equivalent of $2050.

The succeeding 18 years amplify the damage. By the time the man reaches age 61, his spending power would be cut in half once again. Essentially he'd have the spending power of $1025 as he entered retirement (one-quarter of his goal).

The horror comes straight out of a Stephen King novel, because inflation doesn't disappear the moment he retires. It keeps right on chugging, diminishing the value of the dollar during his retirement years as well. If he lives for another 36 years, achieving the ripe old age of 97, he'd have to get by in the latter part of his life on the equivalent of $256.25 per month! (Don't faint; just let the message sink in.) That's what inflation does to the retirement picture.

Rushing to the point, in order to have, 36 years from now, the standard of living that $50,000 per year would have brought when the man was 25, and that would see him through for 36 years of retirement (without spending any principal), our friend would have to plan for a nest egg considerably larger than $500,000. The stunning truth is he'd need six to eight times that much—a tidy three to four million dollars. (Okay, now you can faint.)

IT AIN'T ALL BAD NEWS

The good news needs to be quickly added here. No question about it, we have to plan ahead, but we need not grow overly concerned. Not all of inflation's effects are harmful. Although $3 to $4 million sounds like a fortune, things are not nearly as grim as they might first appear. That sum *also* needs to be understood in terms of the half-life of money. That's $3 million in tomorrow's values, not today's; and there are going to be strong favorable forces at work in your behalf, offsetting many of inflation's negative effects. Some of these forces will occur almost naturally. Others are going to be set in motion by your own efforts as you employ the Wealth Plan.

---

1. Nifty little inflation calculators are available on the Internet. One is found at the Consumer Price Index home page: http://stats.bls.gov/cpihome.htm.
2. U.S. Department of Labor, Bureau of Labor Statistics.
3. Ibid.
4. Taking the 50-year average from 1950 to 2000, inflation averaged very close to 4 percent per year.

CHAPTER 11

Defining the Destination

Comic Lily Tomlin said, "When I was young I wanted to grow up and be somebody. I see now that I should have been more specific." With perspectives about inflation and future purchasing power in place, we are now prepared to sharpen our focus on our destination. Taking a cue from Ms. Tomlin, we need to be as specific as possible and derive a solid answer to the question, *"In today's dollars, what annual income will I need to provide my retirement lifestyle?"*

HOW MUCH IN TODAY'S DOLLARS?

Suppose for a moment that inflation ceased and the purchasing power of the dollar would remain constant. Thinking in terms of what a dollar buys today, how much money would you need annually to cover your retirement lifestyle? As you ponder that question, you're led to consider several important sub-questions. For example, where do you plan to live? Cost of living, tax rates and housing costs vary throughout the country. You can live a lot more cheaply in North Dakota than you can in the Bay Area of California.

You may want to also include these considerations:

1. Do you intend to own your residence(s) or rent it (them)?[1]
2. If you plan to own the home, will you have it paid for?

3. How much traveling do you plan to do? Will you eat out a lot?
4. How many cars and recreational vehicles are you going to own?
5. How much will health care and medical insurance cost?
6. How much will income tax, property taxes, and insurance be?

You may also ask yourself, "What expenses are likely to go up?" Health care is surely one. Travel and entertainment may also increase (at least for a while). "What expenses are likely to decrease?" Generally, income taxes decline because we earn less. Housing costs decline because the mortgage is paid or we move to smaller quarters. Life insurance premiums abate because most policies are paid up by 65. And, a lot of job-related expenses—commuting, business attire, dry cleaning, personal care, lunches—decrease as well.

Do a bit of research. Ask around. Talk to some people who are retired. Although most retired people are reluctant to tell you how much they have put away and what their sources may be, most of them are happy to honestly tell you what it costs to maintain their standard of living. It happens to be one of their favorite subjects, and your biggest challenge won't be to get into the conversation but rather how to *get out* of the conversation when you want to move on. Seriously, a few polite conversations with a few retired people will prove valuable. You may want to include the questions mentioned above in your "interviews" with your retired acquaintances.

It's important to be thorough in your thinking. A lot rides on the answer, so do your "due diligence."

A GENERAL GUIDELINE

Many retirement planners use a simple rule to help their clients answer the question about retirement income—70 percent of current income. But the further you are from retirement, the less useful this hint tends to be. For example, my daughter and son-in-law are just starting out in life. They haven't even begun to reach their earning apex (at least I hope not). For them, the planners' rule would be misleading. They're better off following the recommendations I've outlined above, and make an estimate based on their research. On the other hand, if you happen to be within 10 or 15 years of retirement, the 70 percent rule my be useful.

HOW MUCH IN TOMORROW'S DOLLARS?

Once you've made your decision, you're ready to convert your desired income (in today's dollars) into inflation-adjusted *(tomorrow's)* dollars. For ease of reference we'll call your inflation-adjusted income your DFI (Desired Future Income).

When it comes to estimating our DFI, a variable we must consider is the length of our retirement. None of us knows precisely how long he or she will live, but we *do* know that people are living longer than they did in previous decades. Since we're likely to have a longer retirement, and because inflation doesn't stop at the "traditional" retirement age of 65, I recommend that we extend the focal point of our DFI estimates by ten years—to age 75, rather than age 65. Extending our horizon by the extra ten years provides more cushion and a more accurate estimate of the income we'll need to support the retirement we desire.

To find your DFI please consult Table 11-1. (Fasten your seat belt, you may be in for a jolt.)

Table 11-1

Inflation-Adjusted Annual Income (Age 75)*

	Desired Annual Retirement Income (Today's Dollars)								
Current Age	$40,000	$50,000	$60,000	$70,000	$80,000	$90,000	$100,000	$110,000	$120,000
25	274,000	343,000	411,000	480,000	549,000	617,000	686,000	754,000	823,000
30	226,000	283,000	339,000	396,000	453,000	509,000	566,000	622,000	679,000
35	187,000	233,000	280,000	327,000	373,000	420,000	467,000	513,000	560,000
40	154,000	192,000	231,000	269,000	308,000	346,000	385,000	423,000	462,000
45	127,000	159,000	190,000	222,000	254,000	286,000	317,000	349,000	381,000
50	105,000	131,000	157,000	183,000	210,000	236,000	262,000	288,000	314,000
55	86,000	108,000	130,000	151,000	173,000	194,000	216,000	238,000	259,000
60	71,000	89,000	107,000	125,000	143,000	160,000	178,000	196,000	214,000
65	59,000	73,000	88,000	103,000	118,000	132,000	147,000	162,000	176,000

*Table assumes an average 4% inflation rate

For many of us, especially those in their 20s and 30s, the inflation-adjusted number or DFI—may truly be future shock. Keep in mind that Table 11-1 shows the desired income in *tomorrow's dollars,* not today's. Once that's understood, the number won't seem so daunting. For one thing, the figure that's blowing your mind must be tempered by the "Shirley Deaton Whole Milk Factor."

THE SHIRLEY DEATON WHOLE MILK FACTOR

(I'm glad you asked.) The Shirley Deaton Whole Milk Factor has to do with the "relativity of money." Although it's hard to believe right now, 30 years from now an annual income of $200,000 will seem as commonplace as $50,000 does today. Right now $200,000 seems like a very healthy income, but 30 years will change that perspective.

That's where the whole milk factor comes in. In the early 1960s, when I was in my early teens, I remember riding in a car with my parents, Jim and Shirley Deaton, who were discussing finances. My mother (not Jim, the other one) was upset because the dairy people had just raised the price of whole milk from $1 per gallon clear up to $1.04 per gallon.

Right now that doesn't seem like a big deal. That's because our mind-set about the price of milk is adjusted to present reality. The difference between $1 and $1.04 seems laughable, and that's the point. Back then, four cents bought something. To my parents, this was a big price jump. Today, four cents doesn't buy anything.

Now picture this, keeping in mind that in the '60s milk came in a sterile glass bottle and was delivered right to the doorstep. Imagine Shirley's brilliant little son piping up with something like this: "Mom, I've seen the future—milk doesn't come in a glass bottle any more, and they don't deliver it to your doorstep either. You have to go to the grocery store and get it yourself. It's always on the back wall of the store, and it comes in a plastic container (smeared with some unspeakable goo). Along with the goo, Mom, there'll be some weird black stripes stamped on the container. When you take the milk to the check-out stand, the clerk waves the container over a red light and right before your eyes—like on a TV screen, Mom—they'll tell you that a gallon of milk costs $4!"

If my dear mother could have possibly believed this bizarre story, when she heard that milk was $4 per gallon, her scream of agony would've shattered every window in the car. To her in the '60s, $4 for a gallon of milk would have been an outrage. Today, if you live in California, you're thinking, "Where can I find milk that cheap?"

To complete the picture, consider that my father earned a good middle-class income in those days, bringing in $9,000 to $10,000 a year. If, at that time, my parents had been doing *their* calculations for retirement, their future income needs would have read "$45,000 to $50,000" per year, and they would have choked. In the '60s, $50,000 was a movie star's income. But, guess what? That's precisely what happened. Fortunately, because my parents lived the principles in the Wealth Plan, the refrigerator's been full of goo-covered jugs of $4-a-gallon milk.

OUR NEST EGG IN TOMORROW'S DOLLARS

Now that we're getting used to the altitude of tomorrow's numbers, we can take direct aim on a meaningful long-range goal—the size of the nest egg or FP (Future Principal) that you'll need in order to generate your DFI. Refer to Table 11-2 below to identify your long-range goal—your FP.

Table 11-2

	Desired Annual Retirement Income (Today's Dollars)								
Current Age	**$40,000**	**$50,000**	**$60,000**	**$70,000**	**$80,000**	**$90,000**	**$100,000**	**$110,000**	**$120,000**
25	2,743,000	3,429,000	4,115,000	4,801,000	5,486,000	6,172,000	6,858,000	7,544,000	8,230,000
30	2,263,000	2,828,000	3,394,000	3,960,000	4,525,000	5,091,000	5,657,000	6,223,000	6,788,000
35	1,866,000	2,333,000	2,800,000	3,266,000	3,733,000	4,200,000	4,666,000	5,133,000	5,599,000
40	1,540,000	1,924,000	2,309,000	2,694,000	3,079,000	3,464,000	3,849,000	4,234,000	4,619,000
45	1,270,000	1,587,000	1,905,000	2,222,000	2,540,000	2,857,000	3,175,000	3,492,000	3,810,000
50	1,048,000	1,309,000	1,571,000	1,833,000	2,095,000	2,357,000	2,619,000	2,881,000	3,143,000
55	864,000	1,080,000	1,296,000	1,512,000	1,728,000	1,944,000	2,160,000	2,376,000	2,592,000
60	713,000	891,000	1,069,000	1,247,000	1,425,000	1,604,000	1,782,000	1,960,000	2,138,000
65	588,000	735,000	882,000	1,029,000	1,176,000	1,323,000	1,470,000	1,617,000	1,764,000

*Table assumes an average 10% rate of return on principal

Again this is *future* principal—the number, in *tomorrow's* dollars, that'll be needed to meet your desired lifestyle goal. This must now become your prime financial target—kind of the North Star that helps you set and maintain course.

In my seminars, people's reactions to these numbers—their DFI and FP vary widely. Some people are excited about getting their long-range goals pinned down, and are ready to move forward and achieve them. Others are shocked and unsure as to whether they can attain such lofty-sounding targets. If you're in the latter category, let me offer a word of encouragement. The very factor (inflation) that's made these numbers look so scary is also going to work in your favor as you work your way to your FP goal—provided you heed the principles set forth in the Wealth Plan.

If you're gainfully employed, inflation isn't as harmful as it is for those on fixed incomes. During your lifetime, inflation has been eating away at the dollar, yet you've been able, relatively speaking, to keep pace or exceed its effects. Wages for productive workers historically tend to outpace the ravages of inflation. Look back at my father's situation. In the '60s he was making $10,000 a year as a civil engineer, and paid $1.04 for a gallon of milk. As he reached the apex of his career he was making ten times what he made in the '60s—$110,000 to $120,000 per year, and paying $3 for a gallon of milk. He was much better off even though he spent more dollars on milk. Inflation had not only changed the price of milk, it had also changed the price of labor and services. In some respects inflation had actually been an ally for him.

When we *stop* working, and have to survive on a *fixed* income, inflation then becomes a formidable foe. However, being aware of that fact allows us to prepare for the future by implementing the measures to ensure happy days ahead. Even if your DFI is a shock, aren't you glad that you've been awakened? Knowledge is power, and seeing your goal in specific terms puts you way ahead of the masses of humanity who've never stopped to consider what it will really take for them to know a solid, worry-free future.

---

1. You may want to run a "rent-versus-own" scenario on one of the financial calculators available on the Internet. An example of one can be located at www.kiplinger.com.

CHAPTER 12

Adding Some Good News

Unless you're just starting out, you probably have anywhere from "a bit" to a "truckload" of good news to factor into your future financial picture at this point. If you've been working, you have some Social Security benefits accruing (that's the "bit"). And, if you've been setting aside some money in some type of retirement account—an IRA, a 401(k), or some other type of freedom account—you have even more going for you (that's the "truckload").

A BIT MORE

If you're doubtful about Social Security's future, you're not alone. A reputable poll reported that more Americans believed in the reality of UFOs than in the viability of the Social Security fund.[1] That might be taking it a little *too* far but, clearly, caution is advisable. The less you depend on Social Security for your freedom years, the better off you'll be.

That said, if you want to factor Social Security benefits into the future equation, here's how. As you've probably noticed, Uncle Sam sends out an annual statement of your Social Security account at the end of each year. Upon receiving it, the first thing to do is to verify the accuracy of the statement. Compare your statement with the contribution amount specified on the W-2 form that you received from your employer—the one you file with your federal tax form. I know it'll come as a big shock to you, but the Social Security Administration has been known to err once in a while, and mistakes are more easily corrected along the way than when you've begun to draw benefits.

COST-OF-LIVING INDEXED

Here's another piece of good news. Social Security benefits are *cost-of-living indexed,* meaning benefits are adjusted periodically to keep pace with inflation. As inflation erodes the purchasing power, Uncle Sam increases the number of dollars paid as benefits, thus keeping the relative purchasing power of our benefits substantially the same. If the government continues to keep its promise, the indexing feature of Social Security gives all of us one thing less to worry about. (I don't imagine that comforted you much.)

To get an idea of how much of your DFI (and your FP) Social Security may provide, simply divide your estimated benefit (as stated on your most recent statement) by your desired annual income (your estimate from the previous chapter). For example, let's say that your Social Security benefit is projected to be $10,000, and that your estimated freedom income—in today's dollars—is $50,000 per year. Your calculation would be a simple matter of division:

$$\frac{\$10{,}000}{\$50{,}000} = 20\%$$

In today's dollars your benefit would amount to a fifth of your desired income.

Now, if Uncle Sam keeps his promise and continues to increase benefits in pace with inflation, the percentage should stay relatively constant. Social Security would essentially provide the same percentage of tomorrow's income—in this case, 20 percent. That would also translate over into the lump sum amount you'd need for the future. You could consider that 20 percent of that amount would be covered by Social Security, and that you'd be responsible to account for the remaining 80 percent.

Of course, if you believe that Social Security is sure to collapse before you get to retirement, then all of this is moot, and you should just plan on shouldering the full responsibility. Then, if you *ever do* receive some help from Social Security, so much the better.

ANOTHER POSSIBLE SOURCE OF GOOD NEWS

Are you entitled to pension income? If so, here are a few things to consider: First, is your pension cost-of-living indexed or not? Some pensions are indexed and others are not. If your pension is one that is indexed, you can perform essentially the same type of computation as just described for Social Security. That'll show you how much of a difference your pension will make on your DFI and FP goals.

If your pension is paid out in a fixed amount, and not indexed, then the value of your asset will diminish over time. Even so, your benefit is still better than a summer cold, and can be factored into your freedom picture. Just subtract the annual amount from your future goal. That will give you a realistic picture of its impact on your future. If, for example, you have a pension of $3,000 per month, you can subtract $36,000 from your DFI.

PERHAPS THE BEST NEWS YET

If you've already been saving for your financial future, you're in for more good news, especially if you still have a good chunk of time to harness. The savings you've already accumulated are going to grow. Compounding is going to add value, and to see how much, do the following: Total your current freedom/retirement savings. If you have an IRA, a 401(k) and/or other savings earmarked exclusively for retirement, add up the current value of those accounts.

To see where you really stand—how close or how far you are from your freedom goal—we just have to convert your total current savings to its future value. Begin by finding the appropriate *compounding factor* for your situation by referring to Table 12-1 on the following page.

Table 12-1: Compounding Factor

Compounding Factor (compounded annually)								
	Rate of Return							
Years to your goal	5%	6%	7%	8%	9%	10%	12%	14%
5	1.28	1.34	1.40	1.47	1.54	1.61	1.76	1.93
10	1.63	1.79	1.97	2.16	2.37	2.59	3.11	3.71
15	2.08	2.40	2.76	3.17	3.64	4.18	5.47	7.14
20	2.65	3.21	3.87	4.66	5.60	6.73	9.65	13.74
25	3.39	4.29	5.43	6.85	8.62	10.83	17.00	26.46
30	4.32	5.74	7.61	10.06	13.27	17.45	29.96	50.95
35	5.52	7.69	10.68	14.79	20.41	28.10	52.80	98.10
40	7.04	10.29	14.91	21.72	31.41	45.26	93.05	188.88

First, decide how many years you have for your money to grow before you reach your desired retirement age. Then determine the *average rate of return* you expect on your retirement accounts over the coming years. Be conservative. In the 1990s, it wasn't unusual to average 12-15 percent per year on the funds deposited in a 401(k). From a historical perspective, however, growth that robust is unprecedented, and you may not want to bank on consistently averaging returns that high.

Now locate the row and the column that correspond most closely to your estimates. Your compounding factor is the number you find at the intersection. To forecast what your current nest egg will look like when you've reached your desired retirement age,[2] multiply your current savings total by your compounding factor. By comparing your forecast to your FP, you can assess your current position and get an idea of whether you're on track or not.

There you have it. You have gained some clarity as to your financial future and where you stand. For some of you this may be terrific news and very reassuring. I hope that's the case. If it's not, at least you have been forewarned. And that's good news too, because you can take action, accelerate your savings pace and improve your situation. And, The Wealth Plan will provide many useful ways of enhancing your situation, whatever it may be.

NOTES

1. Frank Luntz and Mark Siegel, "Social Security: The Credibility Gap," *Third Millennium Survey,* September 1994, (October 10, 2000).
2. This estimate, of course, is predicated on actually achieving the rate of return you've estimated.

Section IV

Some insights are just timeless. Take, for example, Emerson's words, "Money can be an obedient servant, but it's a harsh taskmaster." A major objective of this book is to delineate the principles that'll empower you to be on the right side of that equation—to govern your money so that it's not governing you. To enjoy the full spectrum of money's service, we must subscribe to a sound plan based on tried-and-proven practices called the Wealth Plan.

CHAPTER 13

The Wealth Plan
Step 1: Own a Powerful Mind-Set

Great and noble people are strong-minded. They can generate more than a list of good intentions. They've developed the moral muscle to convert good intentions into action, and action into worthy results. They've cultivated the ability to envision what they want, focus on it, commit to it, and then work unflaggingly until they bring their vision into reality. In a nutshell, they're *self-disciplined.*

A few of my friends have coached me to avoid this subject, or at least disguise or sugar-coat it. They've told me that a chapter on discipline will kill my chances of this book ever becoming a best-seller. "People don't want to hear that. Although people sense down deep that it's true, they'd rather hear that there's a quick, easy path to riches, even if it's a lie," said one of my associates. "If you tell them that it comes down to discipline, they'll run from you like you were a tax auditor."

Letting the chips fall where they may, I'm not going to patronize you by sugar-coating what ought to be the most exciting and rewarding journey we'll ever undertake—the journey to impeccable self-mastery. Time has not diminished the wisdom of Henry Emerson Fosdick's statement, "No life ever grows great until it is focused, dedicated and disciplined."

It's not until we embrace discipline, seek to cultivate it, and harness its incomparable power that we really discover how great we can be and how much we can accomplish. The sooner we fully accept that there's no excellence without effort, the sooner we become, do, and have what we seek.

USE MONEY AS A METER

My grandmother had a knack for translating complex issues into clear comprehensible terms. When I was a boy, the subject of discipline came up, and she said something that's stuck with me over the years: "You've mastered yourself when you can hear something bad about another person, and not spread it; when you can receive injury or insult, and not return it; and when you can have money in your pocket, and not spend it."

The most telling of the three may well be the last. I know people who can comply with lofty standards of conduct in virtually every aspect of life, but who are totally out of control when it comes to money. My grandmother went on to say, "You can tell a lot about a person's character by how they earn their money, and how they use it."

As mentioned in earlier chapters, very few people ever amass much money without practicing sound self-management principles. And those who *do* enjoy a sudden windfall will find it only a temporary flare if they lack discipline.

In a real sense money serves as a meter to gauge our growth in this all-important dimension of life. Furthermore, it's about the best "gym" we can find for "working out" and expanding our internal muscle on practical everyday basis. If we set up a system of financial goals and milestones along with a plan to achieve them and then hold ourselves accountable and fulfill that plan, we've had to exercise solid discipline. Every day that we work our plan represents a successful disciplinary work out. Link thirty such days together and we've lived a disciplined month. Before long a practice becomes a habit, and a habit becomes part of our character.

So when it comes to money there's no substitute for discipline and, when rightly viewed, the converse is also true: When it comes to discipline there's no substitute for money. The two go hand in hand. If you want to develop and maintain high levels of discipline, master correct monetary principles. If you want to really own money and make it your servant, master correct self-management principles. We can look at it either way; building one builds the other.

AN ENLIGHTENING INTERVIEW

Not long ago, I had a meeting with a gentleman whose reputation for achievement in his field is virtually legendary. When I arrived at his office, he was just concluding a meeting with one of his assistants. As the young man departed, I was invited to sit down. My host looked across the desk and said, "If people would just quit whining, grab their problems by the throat and attack them, they could make ten times the progress!" From this atypical introduction, I instantly knew that this was going to be a stimulating interview. And I wasn't disappointed.

Explaining what precipitated the comment, my host described how his assistant had made a commitment, but things hadn't gone as expected. Now the young man was rationalizing and looking for ways to excuse himself from the commitment. My new friend went on to state, "If he'd just let the commitment stand—quit trying to wiggle out of it, and just go to work, he would succeed. What's more, he'd be stronger and better for it."

As we exchanged ideas and experiences I was strongly impressed with the forceful mind-set of this man. His high standard of personal integrity was clear and real. Now that you have an idea of his character, let me add that this man is extremely well-to-do financially. He is rich by almost anyone's standards, and I hold that there's a cause and effect relationship between his character and his success.

SOMETHING MONUMENTAL

"People have to learn to keep promises and commitments," he continued. "I don't dare *not* keep my promises—whether to myself or another person. There's no difference, really. Every lapse weakens your character, and makes it that much harder to conquer the next rationalization. Before you know it, you've rationalized yourself into mediocrity, or worse." I was impressed with how seriously he viewed even "small" promises. He seemed to be an anachronism, the last vestige of an out-moded era.

At one time, a person's word was a *binding contract.* People did not make promises, contracts, or commitments lightly—they thought about them carefully. Once made, those pacts were in force until the covenant was fulfilled. Contracts were not made to be broken for gain, or expediency, or simply for convenience, as is so often the case today. Technical loopholes, through which one might squirm, were totally beside the point. They were personally untenable—even reprehensible. Karl G. Maeser, founder of Brigham Young University, expressed it eloquently:

> I have been asked what I mean by "word of honor." I will tell you. Place me behind prison walls—walls of stone ever so high, ever so thick, reaching ever so far into the ground—there is a possibility that in some way or another I may escape; but stand me on the floor and draw a chalk line around me and have me give my word of honor never to cross it. Can I get out of the circle? No. Never! I'd die first![1]

I came away from this interview with reinforced realization that strong moral fiber is *not* the relic of some bygone era. Instead, it has been and always will be the pathway to genuine success and wealth. Although not widely practiced today, uncompromised integrity still stands as the common trait in every truly great man and woman. Keeping everyday promises is something meaningful, even crucial. Few habits build character and personal power faster than keeping *every* promise.

Something real and definite takes place inside us every time we keep a promise. Keeping promises strengthens us, and it adds power. Literally. We expand our capacity to accomplish bigger and better things. Each promise kept adds, and each failure subtracts. The equation is direct and proportionate. The greater and more difficult the commitment, the greater the degree of empowerment when fulfilled. Keeping great promises brings great rewards, but no promise is too small or insignificant to impact our reservoir of strength.

SIGNPOSTS: SIMPLE AND EFFECTIVE

In the formation of habits, distraction and loss of focus become principal roadblocks to success. Often we don't achieve what we set out to do simply because we forget our commitments amid the "busyness" of life. Here's a simple, effective way of staying focused: Create "strategic signposts." Take a few three-by-five cards and jot down reinforcing ideas related to your goals and commitments. Quotes or principles that inspire you work well. Statements like, "Accumulation, not just acquirement," or "A part of all I earn is mine to keep," can keep you *reminded* of your commitment.

Place the signs in strategic locations, so you'll see them as you go through the day. Post one on your mirror where you shave or apply your makeup, one on the dashboard of your car, one on the door of the refrigerator, one on your desk, one on the inside cover of your organizer, and, maybe most importantly, one on the cover of your checkbook. The consistent repetition pays large dividends and opens the door to the rest of the Wealth Plan.

The signpost technique works well, especially if you keep breathing fresh air into it. After a few weeks the signposts become familiar and commonplace. Change the cards once in a while. Find a new inspirational phrase or put the cards in a different place on the mirror. Change the color of the card or the font. Just taking the time to replace and reposition the signposts every two or three weeks reinforces the commitments.

JOINT AFFIRMATIONS

A second way to strengthen commitment and build tough-mindedness is "joint affirmations." This technique works effectively for couples, but it can also be employed if you're single. Just get a mirror and look whoever you're working with right in the eye and commit to implement the Wealth Plan and your goals within it. Joint affirmations serve to create unity at the outset and maintain momentum as you proceed.

I know from personal experience how useful this technique can be. Until the steps in the Wealth Plan became habits for me and my wife, we held brief "commitment sessions" on a regular basis. We'd look each other in the eye, and I'd start with "a part of all we earn is ours to keep." In turn, she'd reply, "A part of all we earn is ours to keep." I'd respond with, "We won't spend all we earn, or lose what we save." And she'd reaffirm, "Yes! We are going to accumulate, not just acquire!" Maybe it was corny, but it worked.

All of us go through moments of weakness. Mutual commitment helps get us past those moments. Using this simple method, Susan and I worked on our weaknesses and toughened up. Our spending stayed in check, and our savings began, for the first time, to really grow—not just bob up and down.

TWO HEADS, ONE COMMITMENT

Stemming from the emphasis on the word "our," joint affirmations beneficially impact a marriage. Money can be the wedge that divides a couple or the bands that cinch them together. In some partnerships one partner earns quite a bit more than the other. If he or she implies that the money is more "mine" than "ours," the splitting has already begun. Here and there the earner conveys resentment over expenditures by the other. The spender resents being resented. Even in two paycheck relationships the feeling of "mine" and "yours" isn't healthy. When the message, "I can't trust *you* with *my* money," gets implanted into a partnership, the pieces start coming apart in a hurry.

The daily "pep rally" effectively reverses that condition. It reaffirms the partnership—the money is *ours,* and we're going to work as a team to reach our goals. By melding all of your resources, tangible and intangible, you're going to go further and higher than either could go alone.

SUBSTANCE—NOT HYPE; COMMITMENT—NOT WISHES

The first step in the Wealth Plan focuses on commitment for good reason. None of the other strategies work without discipline. Giving in to one's self at the slightest twinge of pain or temptation is the hallmark of the mediocre. The powerful concepts in the remainder of this book will bring you financial strength and prosperity, but only when you put them to work. A firm commitment to cultivating a powerful mind-set precedes and precipitates all the benefits that follow.

---

1. Emerson West, *Vital Quotations,* Bookcraft, Salt Lake City, Utah, 1968, p.167.

CHAPTER 14

The Wealth Plan
Step 2: Own a Savings Plan

Over a period of several years, a good friend of mine has ventured into numerous fields of "investment." He has owned stocks and bonds, put money into treasury bills, and had flings with gold, silver and diamonds. He has been a limited partner in a couple of small business ventures, and has invested in his share of real estate—his pride and joy being a lovely ranch in Wyoming, complete with livestock. In short, he has had his finger in just about every mainstream investment pie in America.

To this friend with broad investment experience, I posed the question, "What's the best investment you have ever made?" He thought about it for a few minutes, then responded: "You know, it's interesting. Several years ago my wife and I decided to set aside $500 a month. We have found we can get along fairly well without that money. It doesn't seem to alter our lifestyle much. As soon as we accumulate $5,000 we roll it into a CD (Certificate of Deposit). We have kept that going with a fair amount of consistency." He summed up with this key remark, "You know, to be totally honest with you, we have done better with that simple program than any investment we've ever made."

His next statement was also very meaningful: "By the time you figure everything into most of my investments—the commissions coming and going, the expenses, the legal fees, the accountants' fees, the taxes, and so on—I've never made any real money in any of those other things. Most of the time, I've actually lost a little. I'm really not what you would call a successful investor."

I appreciated his candor. He may not be a successful investor, but he is a typical one. The truth is, most investors do not make all that much money when all is said and done, despite what they say at the neighborhood parties. Later in this book we'll develop a sound strategy for investing, and we won't leave our long-term investment money in CDs. But don't overlook my friend's message, spoken after years of experience. There is power in simplicity. Master a Savings Plan! Own it!

CREATING A FREEDOM RESERVOIR

In the western states we enjoy the benefits of an ingenious system of water repositories called reservoirs. When the pioneers came to these arid lands, they encountered conditions quite different from what they had known in the eastern river valleys. The territory was parched and the rainfall was sparse and unpredictable. (Except in Arizona. Here things are more predictable—we never have much rain.)

To sustain crops and livestock and make communities possible, the pioneers went up into the mountains and dammed off the streams and rivers, creating lovely man-made lakes. Decades later, these reservoirs still offer much to the valleys below. They are places of beauty and recreation. Fish and wildlife flourish in and around them. They also provide security and peace of mind, for in the summer, when the rain is slight, the stored water supplies our needs. Herein lies a useful metaphor—monetary reservoirs offer the very same benefits. Each of us needs to create a monetary reservoir—a lake of liquid financial security.

The laws for creating reservoirs are simple. When outflow *equals* inflow, you have "river." When outflow is *greater than* inflow, you have "drought." When outflow is *less than* inflow, you create "reservoir." The longer inflow exceeds outflow, the larger the reservoir becomes. *And* once the reservoir has been established, outflow can be equal to inflow and the reservoir stays, along with all its benefits.

This metaphor also illustrates the difference between acquirement and accumulation. Those who focus primarily on acquirement confuse the rain with the reservoir. To secure real peace of mind we must do more than make it rain hard once in a while. We must implement ways of *collecting* and *conserving* that rainfall. In actual practice, we must: (1) live within our income and (2) set and keep a monthly savings commitment.

In light of your freedom or retirement goal, determine a fixed amount or percentage of income that you're going to set aside each month. Following the general principle from *The Richest Man in Babylon,* we'll call this practice the "Ten-Ninety Rule." Pay yourself ten percent (or whatever you've decided) each month, and that comes first. Then we live on the remaining 90 percent.

The Ten-Ninety Rule is potent. Its effects are far-reaching. Although the impact begins modestly, it soon gains momentum. Before you know it, what started out as a puddle becomes a pond, and then the pond becomes a reservoir. Then the reservoir starts filling almost on its own at pleasantly amazing rates.

ENLARGING THE RESERVOIR

Once you've implemented the Ten-Ninety Rule, the logical questions become "Where should the reservoir money be put to work? What vehicles should be utilized to maximize the growth?"

First, if you have not done so already, create a modest emergency fund. Part of your reservoir should be liquid and accessible, held in something like a money market mutual fund. (I'll discuss these later.) Your fund should equal three months' living expenses. If you require $3,500 per month to keep your household going, you should have ready access to about $10,000 in case of an emergency. (And I don't mean a white sale at Mervyn's.)

TAXED VERSUS TAX-DEFERRED

The rest of the money, over and above the emergency fund, needs to be put to work in vehicles that offer you protection from the annoying pest we call income tax. The tax code allows for certain plans, commonly called "qualified" or "tax-deferred" plans to grow without yearly taxation. Taxes are postponed until the time of withdrawal, usually at retirement, between ages 59-1/2 and 70-1/2.
You can't evade the tax man entirely, but you usually come out way ahead if you defer your settlement. In the following chart, you can see why.

Comparing Taxed vs. Tax-Deferred Accounts

	INTEREST = 12%		INCOME TAX BRACKET =33%			
	TODAY	6 YRS	12 YRS	18 YRS	24 YRS	30 YRS
TAXED	100,000	159,000	252,000	400,000	634,000	1.0 Mil
TAX-DEFERRED	100,000	200,000	400,000	800,000	1.6 Mil	3.2 Mil

Assuming we are making 12 percent on our money and we fall into a 33 percent tax bracket, let's compare a tax-deferred account with one where the taxes are paid as we go along. If we put $100,000 in an account that gets taxed every year, we wind up thirty years later with one million dollars. Taxes are paid and we can spend that million any way we want. Sounds good, right?

Look at the alternative. If we put $100,000 in a tax-deferred vehicle, we can postpone our settlement with the IRS until we reach retirement age. At that point, thirty years into the future, we wind up with 3.2 million dollars, but we still owe our taxes. Being in a 33 percent tax bracket, we wind up paying one million in taxes and have a little over two million dollars for ourselves. We came out much, much better by deferring our taxes. Even if our tax bracket in thirty years goes to 50 percent, the tax-deferred account still fares better. We would still have $600,000 more by taking the tax-deferred route.

I think I know your next question. "What are some good tax-deferred vehicles?" Here are three to consider.

1. Qualified Retirement Plans at Work

Putting *pre-tax* money into a qualified salary savings plan at work, like a 401(k) or a 403(b), offers a compelling advantage. We make money on dollars that would have gone to Washington this tax year, never to be seen again, if we hadn't put them into our 401(k). Uncle Sam will eventually get his share, but before he does, we can use those dollars to amplify our nest egg. Since we end up dividing a larger pie in the long run, both we and the IRS come out ahead.

Here's a specific example. Suppose we're in a 33 percent tax bracket and we have $600 per month to invest. If the $600 is invested through our qualified plan at work, the full amount—all $600—goes into the account, and we defer the taxes on that money (along with the future growth) until the time of withdrawal, usually at retirement. Year after year, the full amount generates income, and the growth compounds over time—all growth occurring without Uncle Sam reducing it by annual taxation.

With the pre-tax advantage, we'd have to pay our taxes up front and be content to invest the remainder. Using this same example, we'd have to pay Uncle Sam 33 percent first, sending $200 to Washington, leaving us an initial investment sum of $400 instead of $600. Over the long haul, that makes an enormous difference, as you can see from the following chart:

Pre-Tax Versus Post-Tax

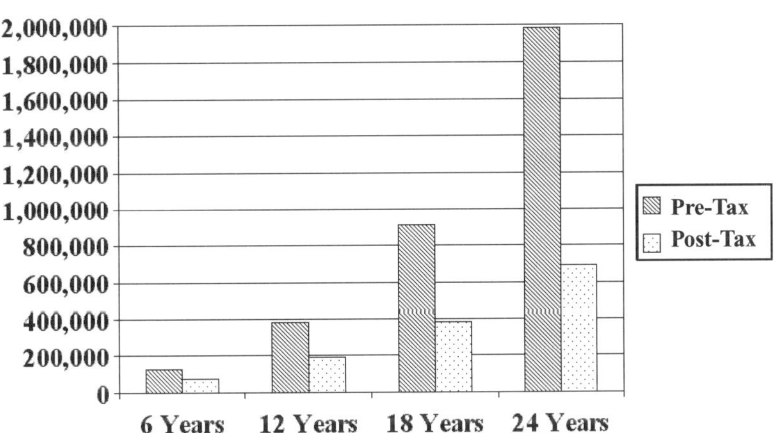

As you see, the difference is substantial. Because the taxed account pays taxes annually, not only do we start with less money in the account, but we also suffer an annual set-back because we have to pay the IRS one-third of our annual gain. Over time, the difference between the two accounts is obvious and dramatic, and the more time involved, the greater the disparity becomes.

By current law, you can save up to 15 percent of your pre-tax income annually, as long as the contribution does not exceed a certain limit. (In 2000 that annual limit was $10,500, but periodically it's adjusted upwardly. You should check with your accountant or tax adviser on the current limit.)

In a qualified plan at work, you're generally offered a menu of different funds from which to select. Later chapters will provide insights to help you choose the right types of funds for your investment horizon. Ordinarily these funds are products of large fund families, like Fidelity, Vanguard, and Invesco, to name just a few of the hundreds. Your money is pooled with money from other investors and thereby carries the name "mutual fund." Usually a mutual fund has a fund manager, who makes an annual commission from you and the other investors for making a bunch of shrewd moves to maximize your return. In the 1990s virtually every fund manager looked like a genius because we had such a robust bull market during that time.

2. Individual Retirement Accounts (IRAs)

Another tax-deferred option is an Individual Retirement Account (IRA). An IRA is not an investment per se. Like your qualified plan at work, an IRA is merely a provision in the tax law, allowing you to invest money without suffering tax consequences every year. Most IRAs are self-directed, meaning that you have the freedom and the responsibility to invest the money any way you choose (within certain limits, which the government has spelled out). Once the money has been put into an IRA, you can put your money into stocks, bonds, mutual funds, certificates of deposits, T-bills, and other investments.

Depending on the size of your income, and other conditions, some or all of your IRA contribution may be tax deductible. Any deductible portion comes right off the AGI—the adjusted gross income—on your tax form.[1] The regulations are full of "ifs and buts," so check with your tax advisor or accountant to see if you qualify. Even if you cannot deduct the contribution, an IRA is still a good idea, offering you a way of putting money to work where the growth is tax-deferred.

THE ROTH IRA

One version of IRA worth considering is the "Roth IRA." Named for the legislator who sponsored it, the Roth IRA offers some attractive advantages. The main feature (providing you meet certain conditions) is that you can withdraw your contributions and the earnings *tax-free*.

The conditions relate to income. The Roth IRA is designed to exclude high-income earners. Eligibility is phased out for individuals with AGI between $95,000 and $110,000, and for married couples with AGI between $150,000 to $160,000. Persons exceeding those limits are ineligible for the Roth IRA but they may still contribute to a traditional IRA.

With a Roth IRA you make non-deductible, after-tax contributions that then grow without further taxation—ever. This feature is especially advantageous to young investors putting money away for retirement. With many years of compounded growth ahead of them, they can wind up with substantial sums in their IRAs. And again the great feature here is that all the growth is *not just tax-deferred,* it's *tax-exempt.* It doesn't get much better than that.

The Roth IRA also offers a good deal of flexibility. Since you've already paid the tax on the contributions, the government allows you to withdraw that money anytime you choose. When you meet certain criteria, you can even withdraw *the growth* on your contributions without paying taxes.

To withdraw the growth on the contributions tax-free, you must have held the Roth IRA for at least five years and be at least 59 ½ years old. The money can be withdrawn by a beneficiary or by the executor of an estate upon the taxpayer's decease. Money can also be withdrawn in cases of disability,[2] and for use as payment of up to $10,000 in acquisition of a principal residence.[3]

Wage earners may contribute to a Roth IRA indefinitely and are never required to take distributions during their lifetime.[4] That means you can take distribution when it suits you—not the IRS. If you choose, you can keep your funds growing in and through your retirement years. The account can even be transferred to beneficiaries who can continue to enjoy the tax-free compounding until they take distribution of the funds. Withdrawals for them would be taxed as regular income at that point.

It should be obvious that the Roth IRA offers significant advantages for the young who do not procrastinate, and make consistent annual contributions. The longer you let your contributions compound, the greater will be the amount you can withdraw tax-exempt. The only thing better than tax-deferred is tax-free, and the Roth IRA offers you that advantage.

ROTH IRAS FOR THE RISING GENERATION

Officially, the government has placed no age restriction whatever on the Roth IRA. So, you're never too young to start accruing the benefits. Well, almost never. You do have to have a job; contributions must be made out of earned income. Convincing the IRS that a two-year old earns income tends to be a hard sell, but for a 12 or 13-year old, who can start a lawn mowing business or who can do baby-sitting on a fairly regular basis, the option certainly exists.

In fact, for a teenager who generates a modest income, a Roth IRA comes close to being the perfect investment vehicle. Remembering that post-tax dollars are invested, if the teenager doesn't earn enough money to be taxed, then he can invest all his money essentially un-taxed, and still reaps the rewards of the tax exempt provision of the Roth, earning a virtually un-taxed windfall at retirement. Note, however, that if the child earns $400 or more through self-employment, a return does need to be filed with the IRS for the payment of social security.[5]

Wanting to get their children off to a turbo-start, some parents and grandparents have their employed children contribute their earnings to the Roth IRA and then gift the children a like amount as "an allowance" or gift. It's a great boon for the children, although teaching them that they can "have their cake and eat it too" may come back to haunt the household some day.

To get and idea of how potent an early-started Roth IRA can be take a look at the following chart:

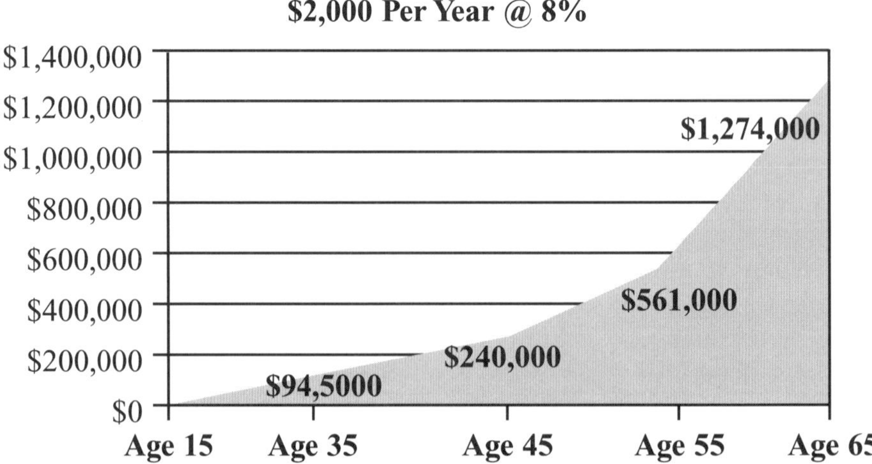

Based on a fairly modest growth rate of eight percent compounded monthly, a young person beginning at age 15, putting $2,000 per year in an IRA, would accumulate an impressive $240,000 by age 45. By age 65, he or she would have over $1,274,000!

3. Tax-deferred Annuities

One other option for tax-deferred treatment is an insurance-related vehicle known as a tax-deferred annuity. Here, money is invested with an insurance company. If you decide to go this route, stick with one of the big name "blue-chip" companies. Avoid small companies that you've never heard of (like Shifty of Scottsdale). Annuities are only as strong as the company you are dealing with.

When you put money into an annuity, you're ordinarily granted a modest death benefit. If you should die before you reach retirement, your beneficiary gets the death benefit or the value of your investment, whichever is greater. The insurance company offers you several choices in how to invest the money. While the growth is occurring, no taxes are due. At maturity you may either elect to "annuitize" (meaning you take your money out gradually) or you may take all the money in one lump sum. There are many options with advantages and disadvantages to each route. Your situation will dictate which is the better choice for you, and a good insurance agent or investment advisor can educate you on your options.

There are two types of annuities to consider, Single Premium and Flexible Premium. Single Premium means you do not "make payments." It is a one-time shot. You simply take a chunk of money (the minimum is usually $10,000), open the annuity, and put the money into investment vehicles within the annuity. Flexible Premium means you start with an initial amount and add to it monthly, quarterly, or annually, as you go along. Your investment options within the annuity are the same as with a single premium version.

THE PRINCIPLE OF CYCLES

Virtually every living organism passes through systematic patterns of growth and change called cycles. The perennial cycle of plants repeats itself rhythmically year after year, adding to the growth of previous years. Each annual cycle (micro-cycle) is a subset of a broader macro-cycle—the overall life cycle of the organism.

The principle of cycles applies to humans as well, although it differs in one key respect. A good part of our growth is discretionary. We have a lot to say about the rate and magnitude of our growth.

Our lives are the sum total of our annual micro-cycles, and we intuitively sense this truth. Near the end of each year, most of us become contemplative and introspective. We evaluate our growth and the progress we've made. Comparing this year's accomplishments to the past, we discern trends of progression or retrogression. Vigorous growth occurs when we make sure the current micro-cycle exceeds the one before, ensuring the expanded potential for even greater growth in the micro-cycles to come.

A METHOD FOR ACCELERATION

If you would like to shift the filling of your freedom reservoir into high gear, try this:

1. Keep a Savings Journal.

Track your savings activity. This record provides a fulcrum for greater self-disciplinary leverage. The example shown on page 101 is a good one because it provides a month-by-month record as well as an annual summary.

2. Record your Monthly Savings for One Year.

For the next twelve months record your savings performance on a monthly basis.

3. Commit to Surpass Yourself Each Subsequent Year.

Compete with yourself. Make a commitment to surpass your previous record for the corresponding month each year. The idea is to hit a new record each month, topping the previous year's all-time high.

IMAGINE THE GROWTH

Picture the internal power this technique harnesses. Visualize yourself, having stretched to a new record, and then unconditionally requiring yourself to shatter that record in the succeeding cycle.

My grandfather once told me, "The biggest reward for doing something hard is that you gain the ability to do something even harder."

I hope that you'll try this idea, and look for other ways to apply it. The full value of this technique won't hit home until you've actually applied it for sixteen to eighteen months. It takes twelve months to complete the first cycle and set your benchmarks. After that, the spirit of internal competition, coupled with the power of keeping every promise, accelerates your success. From then on, the momentum just keeps growing, month after month.

OFFER REWARDS

One more hint: Create a reward system to go along with your savings plan. Predetermine a series of rewards in association with specific savings milestones. For example, when you hit your savings goal three months in a row, reward yourself with a weekend getaway or dinner at your favorite restaurant. At each progressive milestone, make the reward a little bigger and more enticing. Rewards add an element of fun and incentive, helping you to stay on course.

One clarification: Don't take money from your reservoir to fund the reward. Instead, work the rewards into your budget. Never consider your savings, or the earnings on your savings, as spendable until you've achieved the overall freedom goal.

In summary:

CHALLENGE yourself.
MEASURE yourself.
SURPASS yourself.
REWARD yourself.

---

1. Regulations regarding deductibility of IRA contributions change from time to time. Check with your CPA or your tax adviser to obtain the latest version, and to discuss how current regulations may apply to your individual circumstance.
2. The definition for "disability" is lengthy and is also subject to revision from time to time. Check with your tax advisor or the Internal Revenue Service for clarification.
3. The residence may be for the taxpayer, the spouse, a child, grandchild, parent or grandparent. This applies only to those who have not owned a house for at least two years.

NOTES

4. With the traditional IRA a wage earner cannot make contributions after age 70 ½ and also must begin taking distribution by age 70 ½.

5. Currently, 15.3 percent. However, babysitters and newspaper carriers are exempt from the payment of this social security tax.

19____ **SAVINGS JOURNAL** 19 ____

ACCOUNT REGISTER

INSTITUTION	TYPE (CD, Passbook, etc.)	INTEREST RATE	PRINCIPAL	MATURITY DATE	VALUE AT MATURITY OR AT YEAR END

THREE-YEAR SUMMARY

YEAR	TOTAL DEPOSITED	TOTAL WITHDRAWN	NET AMOUNT	NET INCREASE/DECREASE
3 Years Ago: 19 ____				
2 Years Ago: 19 ____				
Last Year: 19 ____				
TOTAL				

MONTHLY JOURNAL

LINE		JAN	FEB	MAR	APR	MAY	JUN
1	Total saved monthly - previous year						
2	Projected monthly goal - current year						
3	Projected increase over previous year (Line 1-2)						
4	Actual monthly savings - current year						
5	Actual increase over previous year						

LINE		JUL	AUG	SEP	OCT	NOV	DEC
1	Total saved monthly - previous year						
2	Projected monthly goal - current year						
3	Projected increase over previous year (Line 1-2)						
4	Actual monthly savings - current year						
5	Actual increase over previous year						

ANNUAL SUMMARY

Projected Annual Savings (Total Line 2) ▶		Actual Annual Savings (Total Line 4) ▶	
		Total Life's Savings at start of current year ▶	
		TOTAL SAVINGS - YEAR END ▶	

CHAPTER 15

The Wealth Plan
Step 3: Own a Tight Ship

"Beware of little expenses; a small leak will sink a great ship," counseled Benjamin Franklin. Monetarily speaking, it is a wonder there are any ships floating at all these days. The liberal use (abuse) of readily available credit is so extensive that it's become a way of life for most people. We're apparently oblivious to the considerable damage inflicted by such profuse leakage.

CREDIT CARD LIVING

Let's suppose that Herb has a credit card with a modest $3,000 limit and has been carrying a balance of about $2,000 for quite some time. He has been making a few charges and making his regular token payments, keeping the balance fairly constant at $2,000. Lately, however, Herb's been tempted to buy a new piece of electronic equipment that runs about $1,000. He reasons that he'll hardly notice the increase in his credit card payment. He's paying that anyway, and a few more dollars won't make much difference. So he does it. He makes his purchase and runs his card up to the $3,000 limit. Simple. Painless. Got what he wanted.

What will it take for Herb to bring his balance back to where it was before the purchase? If he makes the minimum monthly payment required by his credit card—two percent of the remaining balance—and the APR (annual percentage rate) is 18 percent (and many credit cards exact more than that), how much money will Herb have to pay to return his balance to the "original" $2,000? And how many months will it take? Take a guess.

The answers: Herb will pay the credit card company $3,770 and it will take him 79 months! Plus, he will still owe the $2,000! Using credit cards to finance one's lifestyle amounts to psychotic levels of generosity. Can you imagine Herb walking up to the check-out counter with this electronic trinket in his shopping cart and saying to the clerk, "You know, I see the sticker says $999.99, but I just don't feel right about paying you that amount. I'd really prefer to pay you three and a half times that much. How does $3,770 sound?" ("Security...security to the front desk!")

Credit cards are a great convenience when placing orders, or making airline and hotel reservations, but they're *no way of advancing our standard of living.*

THE HIGH PRICE OF INSTALLMENT BUYING

Congress has enacted "truth-in-lending" laws requiring disclosure of the costs involved in installment purchases, but even that doesn't wake people up. They keep blasting holes in their ships like there's no tomorrow. And the truth is: The truth-in-lending form tells *only part* of the truth!

What I'm about to say applies to *installment buying,* not cars. I could have used living room furniture, computer equipment—any number of fun items. I selected cars because they are the most universal purchase.

Suppose Bill, age twenty-five, with $5,000 in the bank and a three-year-old car, which is paid for, goes shopping for a new car. He's looking for something a little "classier"—something with a little more "image." Finding the car that meets his expectations, he drives his hardest bargain with the dealer. They settle on a price of $28,000 for the new car. The dealer, offering him a trade-in of $9,000 on his "old" car, gladly receives Bill's additional $5,000 from his savings, and offers him "easy credit terms" for the remaining $14,000.

At closing, Bill and the dealer sit down to go over the truth-in-lending form. Financing $14,000 at 10.5 percent for five years, Bill's payments come to $300 per month. Bill is elated! He can make those payments, so he's ready to sign, and the truth-in-lending form is a mere formality. Here's what it states:

Principal:	$14,000
Interest Rate:	10.5%
Number of Payments:	60
Monthly Payment:	$300
Total Payments (60 X $300)	$18,000
Less Principal Financed	$14,000
Total Finance Charge	$4,000
Total Cost of Car ($28,000 + $4,000)	**$32,000**

Bill signs the contract and drives away with a shiny new car and a coupon book, thinking that the total cost of the car is $32,000 (assuming no late fees, of course).

Truth-In-Lending is actually a misnomer; the figures tell only the *obvious costs*. Let's look a little deeper. Suppose Will, also age twenty-five, with $5,000 in the bank and a three-year-old car that is paid for, goes shopping for a new car. Suppose also that Will has the same income, lifestyle and expenses as Bill.

Will is aware of Bill's decision to buy the car and make payments. After thinking it over, Will decides to stay with his three-year-old car and leave his $5,000 in the bank. He also reasons that if Bill can get along without $300 per month in his budget, so can he. So Will makes the commitment to add $300 per month to the initial principal of $5,000 in his savings, receiving interest instead of paying it.

At the end of the first year, what's the essential difference in the two men's lifestyles? Not much. They both wrote twelve checks for $300, operating their monthly budgets on the same remainder. (Bill of course enjoyed the prestige of driving a new car for a few months.)

Five years down the road, both men are thirty years old. At that point, what's the essential difference in their lifestyles? Not much. Both drive older cars, and everything on both cars makes noise but the horns. Bill owns a five-year-old car and sixty receipts, and Will owns an eight-year-old car and a hearty little savings account. If we assume that Will made nine percent on his money, he'd have approximately $30,500 in his account

Suppose Will now goes shopping for a new car. Cars have gone up, and the one he selects costs $31,000. The dealer grants a $2,500 trade-in value on his old car, leaving a difference of $28,500. Then the dealer asks, "How much are you going to finance?" Will replies, "Nothing; I'll just pay cash." He withdraws $28,500 from his account and drives away in a new car with no payments to make, and a measly little $2,000 left over.

Now Will reasons, "If Bill can live for the rest of his life without the $2,000 that I have in my account, so can I." How does he know that Bill can live without the $2,000? Because Bill doesn't even know that it exists! Blinded by his desire to own a new car, he's been so busy *paying* interest that he's overlooked the fact that he could've been *receiving* interest. So Will takes his $2,000 and drops it into a broad spectrum mutual fund (more detail later), and just lets it compound for the next thirty-five years. At retirement, neither man even cares about what cars they drove during their twenties and thirties, but Will remembers his mutual fund. So he checks on his account and about faints. His lowly little fund has grown to an impressive $130,000![1]

What did that new car cost Bill—the one he bought at age twenty-five? It cost him $162,000! It cost him the obvious $32,000 and it also cost him the opportunity of making some money on his own money, which in the long run amounted to quite a sum. That's what most of us are not seeing. We don't see the growth potential and the future pay-off of invested money. We go for the immediate gratification, forfeiting the much larger rewards that we could have with essentially the same sacrifice. (Remember, Will and Bill both wrote the same monthly checks—$300.)

People who liberally shell out interest on their lifestyle purchases suffer two hefty penalties. They pay the obvious price of interest, but they also pay an even greater expense in the form of *opportunity* costs. Lost opportunity is by far the most significant, and costs us dearly in the long run. *There's a big difference between what we can pay for and what we can afford.*

Some of us never see that; we keep thinking that if we can "make the payments," then we must be able to "afford it." But we've got to see the bigger picture. It's not just what's leaking, in the form of interest and finance charges, it's what that money could become, if it weren't flowing so freely into someone else's account. Will Rogers said it better than anybody else: "Interest! Them's that understands it, gets it. Them's that don't, pays it!"

THE VALUE OF EARNED MONEY VERSUS BORROWED MONEY

People spend borrowed money less carefully than they do earned money. Borrowed money is hard to value. It doesn't seem that much harder to borrow $14,000 than it does $12,000. Hence we tend to spend more for a car—do less shopping around, less bartering, less discriminating about options and extras, and are not as persistent in negotiating with a dealer—when we finance rather than pay cash.

I learned this lesson through personal experience. One of the first cars I purchased was kind of a splurge, and I financed a large part of it. I was so set on getting the car that I made only half-hearted efforts to hammer on the salesperson and do some bargaining. I wound up getting about every extra possible—the difference in the payments did not seem all that great.

I enjoyed the car, and eventually I did get it paid for. During the period of making payments, I came to realize the concepts I am sharing with you. A few years later, I had saved $35,000 and went shopping for one of those prestigious sports sedans. Passions were percolating during the test drive—the car proved to be everything I had been dreaming about.

Then the negotiations started, and I began to realize the power of the truth: People are *more careful with earned money than with borrowed money*. I had worked hard to earn and save the $35,000. That $35,000 chunk felt good in my account, and the more I thought about taking that whole amount and exchanging it for a car, the more I examined the whole transaction in my mind. I began to weigh things more carefully.

I began thinking, I'm still going to get that car, but I'm not going to pay one cent more than I have to. Perhaps I can get the car and still have some of my cash left over. So I bartered and negotiated. I was proud of myself; I wasn't my usual patsy self. Shopping around, checking the guides, talking to friends in the business, and playing one dealer against the other, I finally got the car down to a great price. And I still couldn't quite bring myself to buy it. I thought the salesperson was going to drop dead when I said, "I'm going to think about it for another twenty-four hours."

On the way home I made my decision. When the passion cooled and I was more rational, I could see that I had better uses for that $35,000. I ended up driving a hard bargain on a car a few steps down from the first one. I gave up $20,000, kept $15,000, and felt 200 percent better about the whole situation. Paying interest is a poor value, and so is overpaying for an item. When we're spending earned dollars, our perspectives are sharper. We sense the real value of the money we're spending. We tend to make better judgments, and we stop many of the leaks that impede our ships.

THE FORTUNE HIDDEN IN YOUR MORTGAGE

Pointing to the fortune that can be made in the burgeoning stock market, some financial authors tell us that we're dumb to pay off our mortgages.[2] Their reasoning (prospector's mentality) may look good on paper but it rests heavily on the assumption that the stock market is going to continue to obediently burgeon. What happens if the market stalls? What happens if it sinks? When such reversals occur,[3] people who are spread thin, extended to the gills, start gasping for oxygen.

My recommendation is to opt for strength over speculation. Consolidate. Minimize risk, rather than amplify it. Remember the adage, "a bird in the hand is worth two in the bush." When we accelerate payments on our mortgages, get out of debt, and eliminate interest, our gains are *real* and enduring. A downturn in the market can't take them away from us. Even during the supposedly carefree days of burgeoning bull markets, some once-stunning portfolios have crumbled within hours as a cherished stock or fund has fallen out of Wall Street's capricious favor

Once we've secured our position, and eliminated debt from our lives, we have more money—mostly angst-free—to invest with, and the gyrations of the stock market are not nearly as threatening or lethal. Even if things were to go south in a major way, our resilience and "staying power" would be far deeper. We could weather the storm. Again, Will Rogers was right on, "You can't break a man that don't borrow." Notably, Will's statement holds eerily-prophetic overtones when we realize that he made it in 1923, six years prior to the great stock market crash that callously devastated all the people who espoused the same highly leveraged ideology being touted today.

The second argument generally offered for not retiring a mortgage centers on tax savings. Some people would rather have a root canal without anesthesia than pay an additional penny in taxes. I'm certainly not advocating extra tax donations, I want to keep my tax bill down too. But sometimes paying a little more tax is actually preferable to what we forego by trying to avoid every iota of tax. In my opinion, this is just such a case. True, we give up some reduction in our income tax when we eliminate the interest deduction, but we more than make up for it by gaining a rather scarce but priceless commodity these days—peace of mind.

Requiting our mortgages produces a substantial chunk of wealth plus it offers us an additional layer of financial strength to our position. People who have secured the roof over their heads sleep better, and they do far less nail-biting when the Dow plunges and the NASDAQ wobbles.

Prepaying principal on long-term loans, like a home mortgage, can amount to sizable interest savings.[6] Let's say we have a thirty-year, $150,000 mortgage at eight and a half percent. The monthly payment is roughly $1,150. By increasing the monthly payment $150 per month, making the payment a nice round $1,300, we'll save over $100,000! The extra $150 goes directly to the reduction of principal, which reduces the amount of interest paid over the life of the mortgage. We pay down the balance much faster, saving a lot of interest in the process. In this case, the loan would be paid off in twenty years instead of thirty, and the interest saved would look like this:

30 years	(360 payments) @ $1,150	=	$414,000
20 years	(240 payments) @ $1,300	=	$312,000
			$102,000

After our mortgage is paid, we can, with no great risk to our lifestyle or overall security, invest the $1,300 per month for the next ten years and still add a healthy sum to our reservoir. At 8 percent compounded quarterly, you would add over $237,000!

"YOU'LL NEVER SEE SAVINGS LIKE THESE AGAIN"

Seems like it should be simple. Saving is saving. Spending is spending. Yet somehow we lose track of this simple logic amid a mass of advertising confusion. The line goes like this: "You can save a bundle right now if you will come right down and spend some money."

If you sit in front of a television for any length of time you will be exposed to that ploy a dozen times. Advertisers have stricken the word spend from the dictionary, banishing it to advertising outer darkness. How many time have we heard something like this:

Ladies and gentlemen, boys and girls, come to our Fourth-of-July, year-end, close-out, going-out-of-business, inventory liquidation, first anniversary, over-stocked, everything-must-go, SALE-A-THON! You have never seen SAVINGS like this before! Everything in the entire warehouse [I was hoping he would say planet] has been marked down! Way, way down! SAVE like never before! With prices like this you cannot AFFORD to wait another minute! Get down here right away! You may never see SAVINGS like these again! Everything has got to go! The SAVINGS are going through the roof! If you're like me, (and I know I am), you won't want to pass up a chance to SAVE THIS MUCH! Pack up the kids, pack up the granny, pack the car, and pack up your troubles in your old kit bag and get down here while the savings last!! This is a once-in-a-lifetime SAVINGS extravaganza! (Did I mention there would be free hot dogs and balloons for the babies?)

As I write this, I can't keep from chuckling. This is not *that* far off the actual scripts I'm trying to parody. I was trying to overplay it for the sake of humor, but I couldn't do it. These pitches are already as over-hyped as a person can make them.

The hucksters use every superlative in the thesaurus but you'll never hear the word "spend." They only and always use *save*. Why do they do this? Because (amazingly) the tactic works. Why do we fall for it? Because (not amazingly) we'd like to believe it can be done—that we could save while we spend.

Too many of us think that money has only one purpose—to be spent. It could be used as a workforce to eventually take our place as the bread-winner, but not many of us see that. We only work to spend. When we do save, we're only working to build up enough cash so we can really unleash the spending. What then would be more wonderful than to be able to do both, simultaneously? We could spend a pile of money so that more money would magically roll in. Such a cycle would allow us to spend again, thus producing a new chunk of savings which could then be spent. (Get another shopping cart, Madge.) Like a perpetual motion machine, we could just go on spending forever.

Getting back to reality, we do ourselves an enormous favor when we restrain our craving to spend every penny we earn. No less than Andrew Carnegie said, "Thrift is the great fortune maker."

If you border on being one of the many "spendaholics" in this nation (and experts estimate that the numbers reach into the millions) let me pass on another suggestion. Cut down on your television viewing. What does TV have to do with spending? When we face reality, we must admit that TV is not an education medium. (It could be, but it's not.) TV is not an entertainment medium or a relaxation medium. We may *think* we are relaxing or being entertained, but when it gets right down to it, we're being sold! Television is an advertising medium pure and simple. And I'm not just talking about the commercials.

GETTING A GRIP

Too many of us chase our lifestyle with our income, instead of providing our lifestyle out of our income. Thoughts such as, "I'll be getting a raise soon," or "I'll be working a lot of overtime in the next few months," or "We'll be getting a big tax refund next April"—any thinking that advocates spending now and catching up later gets us into trouble.

Each of us must get a grip on our tendency to overspend, and reject the debt and deficit spending habit. Setting firm goals and paying ourselves first constitute an effective bulwark against our penchant to acquire. Further along in the Wealth Plan, we'll add more weapons to our arsenal, but *understanding the consequence* of overspending and paying interest reinforces our resolve to employ all these sound measures.

---

1. Assuming an average rate of 12 percent on his $2000, which is a reasonable assumption for a 35-year period.

NOTES

2. Ric Edelman, *The New Rules of Money,* Harper Collins Publishers, New York, 1998, p.53.
3. Again, I said *when,* not *if.*
4. And, again I emphasis, these savings are real. The interest saved does not evaporate when the markets plunge.

CHAPTER 16

The Wealth Plan Step 4: Own a Debt Elimination Plan

Americans, whose forefathers fought and died for freedom, have grown fond of servitude. For many it has become a way of life. Statistics show that debt liability for most families in the United States grows annually.[1] While most people vaguely acknowledge that indebtedness is bondage, few take the definitive steps to banish it from their lives. The majority of our generation will go to their graves never knowing the peace and joy of being totally, completely out of debt.

EASIER TO BORROW THAN REPAY

The shackles of debt slip on ever so lightly, softly, and sometimes very quickly. But once locked in place, nothing but concerted effort can free us from their grasp. That's when we come to appreciate Mohandas Gandhi's observation: "Golden shackles are far worse than iron ones."

Getting out of a quagmire of deep debt takes time, but it can be done, and the sooner we wake up and resolve to free ourselves, the better off we'll be. Therefore, to those who *haven't* fallen into the trap, I say, "Be wary and wise. Avoid debt in every way possible." In my mind, only a few purposes justify incurring debt—a good education and a home. A third purpose might be to start or expand a business, provided the business plan is well-conceived and realistic. However, even for worthy objectives, undertake debt cautiously, prudently and modestly.

I've seen many young people stifle their destinies by over-mortgaging their future through excessive borrowing during their school years. With a little more sacrifice, they could have lessened the debts they undertook considerably. Their journey to pay back the loans would have been much shorter, and their prosperity would have come sooner and been more substantial in the long run. Some people accrue so much debt in their college years that they're forced to play catch up the rest of their lives.

The same principle holds true for home mortgages. Don't stretch yourself to the maximum and "grow into your house and payments." Paying interest does not build equity.

In general, home equity loans are also bad news. Despite all the touted "advantages," frittering away the equity in your home is not wise. Instead of delaying, we should accelerate the attainment of a mortgage-free roof over our heads. Some rationalize by saying Uncle Sam gives them a break on their taxes, lessening the real cost of repayment. Even if Uncle Sam would let you write off every last cent of interest, not just a percentage, the "benefit" still doesn't compensate for the peace of mind and overall financial strength that comes from owning the most important material asset you'll ever have: your own home.

HOW MUCH IS TOO MUCH?

This advice, I realize, may be arriving "post disastrum" (fictitious colloquial Latin is my sub-specialty). If you *know* the you're in deep debt, and are sinking out of sight, you must embark on an immediate and undeviating course of debt elimination, or else declare bankruptcy. If you're uncertain as to how much debt is too much and what you're real debt situation may be, here's an objective way to assess your position.

Over the years, lenders have used a simple guideline for evaluating their clients' debt levels (to the lender they are considered "risk levels"). They calculate a "debt-to-income ratio" for the potential borrower. (This is why borrowers must submit those revealing confession sheets filled with personal disclosures known as financial statements.) The debt-to-income ratio measures the borrower's financial buoyancy. This ratio is easily calculated, and to determine yours, take the following steps:

1. List All Your Debts

Make no exceptions; list them all. You want to clear the table and remove every legal lien on your soul as well as your balance sheet. There is more than meets the eye here—debt has mental/spiritual implications as well as financial.

Do not include regular monthly necessities, such as food, gas, and utilities. Although you pay for them monthly, you're not paying interest on them, and they are to some degree discretionary and not fixed contractual payments. And that's the point. If, in addition to the necessities, you've obligated yourself to a lot of other payments, you have very few dollars left over, and a lender will not lend.

Most home payments include not only principal and interest but taxes and insurance as well. If your mortgage payment does not include those figures, add them to your mortgage payment amount. They are mortgage-related expenses and must be considered part of the debt picture. If you are renting, do not include your rent on the list. We'll deal with that issue shortly.

2. Determine Your Monthly Debt Payment (MDP)

Once you've listed all your debts along with the monthly payment, total the payment column. The total of all payments for all your debts is known as your Monthly Debt Payment, or your MDP.

3. Determine Your Debt-to-Income Ratio

Now divide your MDP by your monthly net income. "Net income" in this definition is all earned income immediately after governmental deduction but before anything else is subtracted. The answer you derive is a percentage or ratio called the debt-to-income ratio.

$$\frac{\textbf{MDP}}{\textbf{Monthly Net Income}} = \textbf{DEBT-TO-INCOME RATIO}$$

EXAMPLE

Total MDP = $800
Total Net Income = $2,000

$$\frac{\$800}{\$2,000} = .40$$

Thus, your Debt-To-Income Ratio = 40%

Lenders have a traditional benchmark for the debt-to income ratio. Most lenders start backing off when the percentage total debt (including the mortgage payment) falls in the neighborhood of 40 percent of the monthly *net* income. People in that position are poor risks because their discretionary dollars are severely limited. They are already headed for Default City.

Lenders also use another general rule known as the "Mortgage Rule," which states that the mortgage payment should not exceed 25 percent of the gross income. Therefore, if you are not presently paying on a mortgage—say you're renting or have your home paid for—your debt-to-income ratio should fall at or under 15 percent of your net income.

Compute your own ratio. If your debt-to-income ratio is *above* 40 percent (15 percent if you are renting), you are skating on thin ice. Reason and prudence beg you to lower your debt; and I am asking you to aspire to having no debt at all!

THE DEBT ELIMINATION PLAN

The Debt Elimination Plan is tried and proven; it works! Once you've mastered the first three steps in the Wealth Plan—that is, you have (1) committed to a firm accumulation mind-set; (2) implemented a monthly savings habit, consistently paying yourself at least 10 percent per month; and (3) kicked the debt and deficit spending addiction—then you're ready for the Debt Elimination Plan. Though it starts modestly, the plan grows steadily into a robust positive force, freeing you from the manacles of debt in a sound and certain manner.

Right now you are obligated to pay a certain amount each month to your creditors (your MDP). Under the debt elimination plan, this amount is going to remain unchanged throughout the process. Following the outlined steps, you will pay off large chunks of debt without impacting your monthly budget or having to increase your income:

1. Accrue No More Debt

NONE. I know this admonition is redundant, but I must emphasize that from this point on, deficit spending is not an option. Be tough; live within your income.

2. Set a Specific Debt Elimination Goal

Look at your debt-to-income ratio. What would you like that ratio to be? You may choose any percentage between zero and 40 percent. I recommend it be not more than 25 percent. In fact, I'd like you to consider totally debt-free living.

3. Use Debt Service Money Exclusively for Debt Elimination

You will achieve your goal using the money that is already going to your creditors. As, one by one, you pay off your debts, more and more money will be "freed up." The "freed" money stays in the debt elimination program until you have reached your goal. The power in the plan comes from using this money to accelerate the rate of repayment on your remaining loans.

Now we get to the heart of the plan.

4. List Debts from the Smallest Balance to the Largest

So far, your debts have been listed in no particular order. Reorganize them now, listing them in order, from the smallest balance to the largest.

5. Divide Your Savings Plan

If you have a high debt-to-income ratio (35 or above), you'll need to modify your savings commitment *temporarily.* If you can avoid this modification, do so. However, if you are stretched to the hilt as it is, you will need to divide your monthly savings amount in half. One half (or five percent of your net monthly income) will still flow into your freedom reservoir. The other half will be used to accelerate debt elimination. Although you slow down the growth of your savings for a time, you are better off eliminating high interest payments. In a high-debt situation, your best investment is debt elimination.

6. Pay Off Your Smallest Debt First

Begin eliminating your debts one by one, focusing on the smallest debt first. Irrespective of interest rate, payment amount, or any other consideration, attack the smallest balance first. The objective is to eliminate one debt and one worry as soon as possible. It also frees up some money (and eliminates the escalating cost of an envelope and one postage stamp each month).

On the smallest debt, pay the required payment plus the five percent you held back from your savings plan. On all the other debts, pay the minimum monthly amount required to keep the account in good standing. Shortly, you will have paid off the first debt, and will have liberated some capital. At first, the plan will look like this:

DEBT ELIMINATION PLAN

1. Debt 1	Regular Payment + 5%
2. Debt 2	Regular Payment
3. Debt 3	Regular Payment
4. Debt 4	Regular Payment
5. Debt 5	Regular Payment
6. Debt 6	Regular Payment

7. Roll All Freed Money onto Debt 2

With you first obligation out of the way, roll that money onto the payment of the next debt on your list (Debt 2) along with the additional five percent, until that debt is paid.

2. Debt 2	Regular Payment + D1 + 5%
3. Debt 3	Regular Payment
4. Debt 4	Regular Payment
5. Debt 5	Regular Payment
6. Debt 6	Regular Payment

8. Continue the Process until You Reach Your Goal

With the elimination of each debt, all the freed money is rolled onto the payment of the succeeding debt. The process continues until you have reached your debt elimination goal. Each time one debt is eliminated, the process accelerates a bit. What begins as a trickle soon becomes a stream and eventually a torrent. By this simple and reasonable technique, hefty amounts of debt can be retired.

ANOTHER APPLICATION OF THE INCENTIVE FORMULA

Previously I recommended a simple success formula that produces remarkable results:

CHALLENGE yourself.
MEASURE yourself.
SURPASS yourself.
REWARD yourself.

This same formula will pay major dividends when applied to the Debt Elimination Plan. Predetermine a few intermediate goals or milestones and establish an appropriate reward for each milestone.

In the case of the Debt Elimination Plan the incentive-bonus system may be even more crucial. I have observed a number of households that were working toward debt elimination. They started well and kept things going for a time. Then (and, interestingly, it's often *just before* paying off a major debt) they lapse into a splurge mode again and march backward several paces. The reward system provides a way of avoiding that pitfall. Tie an appealing reward to the elimination of each creditor. That will get you past the "almost there" splurge syndrome.

To fund your milestone bonuses, allow yourself a little latitude with the freed money. This suggestion differs from my recommendation in regard to the savings plan. When you have completely paid off a major creditor, take a month off. Take the "extra" debt reduction money and do something fun. You may not be able to do much when you reach the first milestone, but that will change. Down the road you'll have a nice sum with which to reward yourself. And the biggest reward of all will be the day you're able to echo

Martin Luther King when he said, "Free at last! Free at last! Thank God Almighty, free at last!"

---

1. General Audit Corporation, The Magnitude of Consumer Debt, September 1997, http://www.generalaudit.com/debt.html (October 24, 2000).
International Credit Association, "National Statistics," Debt Solutions of America, April 1998, http://www.becomedebtfree.com/statistics.html (October 24, 2000).
U.S. Census Bureau, "Banking, Finance, and Insurance," Statistical Abstract of the United States: 1999, December 31, 1999, http://www.census.gov/prod/99/pubs-/99statab/sec16.pdf (October 24, 2000).

CHAPTER 17

A Word About Bankruptcy

Some people who read this book might be in such painful financial straits that it may be virtually impossible to get themselves out. For those who have never been in such a predicament, it is easy to pass judgment. To those of us who have been spared such anguish I say: "Count your blessings. Perhaps there, but for the grace of God, go we all." There are many fine, honest people who through no egregious sin on their part find themselves trapped in a bed of financial quicksand. If you are one of these, I'd like to offer some help.

We live in a great land. There is an inspired system of laws that provide liberty and a reasonable degree of justice for all. Within the framework of the law, fair and legal provisions exist for debt relief. True, abuses occur, but not everyone who seeks protection under those provisions is a criminal or a deadbeat.

Most people abhor the thought of bankruptcy. Yet, when one has no other viable alternative, one might have to proceed with that remedy under the guidance of sound legal counsel. Bankruptcy laws are enacted, in my opinion, precisely for people with sound moral fiber but who have no other reasonable alternative to end their monetary nightmare.

Sometimes even obtaining accurate facts upon which to base a decision is difficult. People in financial distress often hesitate to consult an attorney, because the last thing they need is another bill. Fortunately, most attorneys who specialize in bankruptcy law have a policy of offering an initial consultation free of charge. They'll listen to your story and describe your alternatives. You do not incur a fee until you employ their services to enact one of the alternatives.[1] Despite all the negative lawyer jokes, the majority of them do have a heart, and those who specialize in this area of the law understand your plight. Obtain more than one opinion. If you hear the same recommendation from two experts, you pretty well have your answer.

Different degrees of bankruptcy exist. Frequently referred to as "chapters," each has its separate provisions and limitations. Chapter 7 is full-blown bankruptcy. Chapters 11 and 13 are "partial bankruptcies," allowing you different ways of getting back on your feet without losing all of your assets.

Only you can decide what's right for you. Declaring bankruptcy is a significant decision, and you must consider it carefully. Serious ramifications apply—the blemish on your credit record, for one. As you weigh the issues, you will know whether it's a morally and financially acceptable route for you.

FORECLOSURES

My philosophy regarding foreclosures resembles my position on bankruptcy. Submitting to a foreclosure is not necessarily a flagrant moral transgression. Sometimes, even for responsible people, no other reasonable alternative exists. Again, consult your conscience. Only you can say whether this approach is legitimate or merely a way of shirking responsibility.

Keep in mind that on the deed or in the contract—the instrument you signed to begin the deal—your creditor agreed to accept certain remedies in the event of your failure to uphold your side of the agreement. The creditor agreed to those options at the outset. Letting her or him exercise those options is neither unethical nor immoral, although the situation may not be pleasant for either one of you. Know this, in most states, the law is on the creditor's side in such cases.

Responsible communication on your part strengthens your position. Most people are fairly reasonable and understanding, and sometimes things can be renegotiated. Be sure to seek out all your options before you finalize a decision. Enduring a foreclosure also has its consequences. This defect damages your credit rating as severely as a bankruptcy. In fact, in some cases it is considered worse.

ABOUT CREDIT RATINGS

The foregoing leads us to a discussion of credit records and credit ratings. First, be clear that a spotless credit rating is a valuable asset—one to be achieved and preserved. A strong credit rating increases your financial options. If you do have a good credit record, keep it.

Those who are debating alternatives such as foreclosure or bankruptcy, need to know that credit scars are not easily corrected. They linger for at least seven years. That isn't the end of the world either, but you'll live with that record for close to a decade.

Before moving on, let's talk about credit repair agencies. I refer to the firms who claim to be able to clear your record (for a not so "very small fee"). My advice: "Lock up your purse, Gladys, and head for the car." Don't get involved with them. They can legally do nothing for you that you can't easily do for yourself. If the items on your record are incorrect, you can rectify them yourself. Clerical errors can be cleared within a few weeks by obtaining written verification from the creditor, which you can usually obtain with a phone call. You don't need to pay a third party to accomplish that. If the information is correct, no legal way exists to expunge the blotch.

REBUILDING CREDIT

If your credit rating is defaced and imperfect, all is not lost. You can get yourself back into fairly good terms with the world in about two years. Here is how:

1. Establish Unwavering Discipline in Your Life

Until you establish some self-discipline, a poor credit rating can actually be a blessing. Easy credit has been your downfall. Having no other alternative but to "pay as you go" may well be the beginning of your rehabilitation.

On the other hand, once you have overcome this weakness you must demonstrate that by living within your means and paying every bill promptly. As you proceed to reestablish your credibility with the world, any flaws here will be lethal. Stay current and pay on time!

2. Own a Savings Plan

Establish a savings account and add to it faithfully each month. That record in itself tells a potential lender that you're exercising a bit of discipline. Your savings pattern also opens the door to another useful tool, a passbook loan.

3. Obtain a Savings Passbook Loan and Repay It

Once you've established a savings track record and amassed a modest sum in your savings account, you can obtain a loan, using that money as collateral. This is called a "Passbook Loan." Suppose, for example, you have $3000 in your savings account. You could borrow $1500 with no questions asked, because your savings serve as collateral for the loan. Until the loan is repaid, your account is frozen, and the bank has rights to it, if you default. Despite your poor credit history, banks make these loans because they incur no risk. Terms and conditions vary, so shop around, making sure that the bank you select reports regularly to the credit agencies.

Obtain the loan and make every payment on time—flawlessly. Make sure each payment arrives a day or two ahead of the deadline, and continue this pattern for six months or so—enough time to show up on your credit record. Once you're sure your timeliness appears on your credit report, pay off the rest of the loan early.

If you can afford to do so, apply this procedure at two different banks at the same time (but don't overburden yourself). The more entities reporting your good performance, the better.

4. Obtain a Credit Card

Another way of reestablishing a good credit rating is through the responsible use of a credit card. In the same way you obtained your passbook loan and for the very same reasons, most banks will issue you a credit card. Again, your savings account will be frozen, and the credit limit on the card will be set below the amount in your savings account.

Use the card for a few purchases each month. It is imperative that you do not exceed the limit and that you pay the entire balance off each and every month. A clean payment record on a major credit card is one of the fastest ways to reestablish your credit rating, because this record provides a broadly-accepted credit reference.

5. Monitor Your Credit Record

You cannot afford another glitch on your record. From this point on your performance must be flawless and your record must be spotless. It's amazing how often mistakes are made on credit reports, and someone else's blunders wind up on the wrong record. The similarity in names, transposed digits on a Social Security number, or any number of other errors can occur. Keep an eye on your record. You have the legislated right to know your record and who's reporting or requesting information from your file. Exercise that right, and check your credit report once a year. Contact one or two of the larger credit systems, such as Experian, Equifax or Trans Union.[2]

By following these suggestions, you can achieve a good credit status within a couple of years. When you achieve it, keep it!

---

1. Obviously, verify the free consultation policy as you set the appointment.
2. Experian, Box 9595, Allen, TX, 75013. 888-397-3742. www.experian.com. Equifax, Box 105069, Atlanta, GA, 30348. 800-290-8749. www.equifax.com. Trans Union, Box 2000, Chester, PA, 19022. 800-888-4213. www.transunion.com.

CHAPTER 18

The Wealth Plan Step 5: Own a Money Expenditure Plan

Some people don't like to say dirty words. Some people don't like to hear dirty words. Some people don't like to read dirty words. *Budget* is not a dirty word. But you'd sure think it was, the way so many folks experience severe power outages when they hear the word budget.

In my seminars, to get around this mental blockade, I state, "Wealthy people have mastered a money expenditure plan." The audience is momentarily thrown off balance. They are not completely sure what I mean, and they dutifully write the phrase "money expenditure plan" into their workbooks. Many actually seem quite impressed with it—it sounds rather sophisticated. Not until they've opened their minds a bit do they discover the punch line—that a money expenditure plan means "a budget."

If you are one of the multitude who have tried a budget and have only succeeded in discovering the depths of frustration, take heart. I understand; I've been there too, and working through some of the frustrations with budgeting, I've discovered a few things that can make a big difference.

The initial step is mental. Before we do anything else, we need to see that living by a budget plan is the strongest, quickest way to reach our goals, and that many of the negative ideas we hold about budgets are invalid.

Misconception No. 1: A Budget Is Slavery

"A budget is slavery in print. It robs me of my independence. I don't want to be bound to some piece of paper. I want the freedom to spend my money how I want, when I want."

Reality: A Budget Is the Gateway to Freedom

We need to be careful about what we label "freedom" and what we label "slavery." Addicts are famous for their misuse of these terms. They're continually pleading for their *freedom,* while being tragically enslaved by some harmful habit. Similarly, the hue and cry of the morally anemic amounts to the same deception—that adherence to standards constitutes slavery. In actuality, living by lofty standards and practicing high levels of personal discipline open the vistas of possibility and real freedom of choice.

Addicts have bad habits, and addictions come in many forms. Spending without planning is a bad habit. People who don't want to be "slaves" to a rational plan of their own making are likely to become "slaves" to their splurges and excuses. We don't achieve financial freedom until we live on less than we make, separate needs from wants, vanquish debt, and build up surplus cash. Accomplishing those rewarding goals is *very* difficult to do without a well-structured plan.

Misconception No. 2: A Budget Only Applies to Low-Income Nerds

"A budget is for unimaginative bean-counters—the kind of people that do not and never will have big money. When you have good money rolling in, you can spend all you want and you still have money left over. A budget is for methodical types who can't see the big picture."

Reality: A Budget Is an Essential Tool for People with Vision

Financial freedom is not a state of money. In reality it's a way of living, that has, at its core, clear objectives and perspectives. People who achieve financial freedom don't rely on luck or fate. They have vision—they know where they are going and how they'll get there. They won't allow passion to overpower purpose. They make sure their long-range objectives are the governing forces in their monetary affairs. Hence they create a budget as a means of controlling their destiny and realizing their goals.

Misconception No. 3: A Budget Is Drudgery

"Life on a budget is boring. It's a life of no hits, no runs, no fun. There is no room for spontaneity. I may never be rich, but at least I am going to enjoy what little money I get."

Reality: A Budget Is Great Sport

If you love sport and competition, you should love the challenge of a budget. Sports are popular because you keep score. The scoreboard gives immediate feedback on who's winning and who's losing, and the players use that information to adjust their performance and thereby alter the course of the game. A budget serves the same purpose. We use it to monitor our progress—quickly assess successes and failures, so we can make adjustments. Thus, our progress accelerates.

A BUDGET FORM IS NOT THE BUDGET

I have talked with dozens of people who are attempting to achieve financial freedom without a budget. When I ask why, I usually hear the same response: "I've tried one and it didn't work." With further questioning, I usually uncover more or less the same scenario. They talk about picking up a package of budget forms at a grocery store—the one titled "Monthly Budget." Devoting the better part of a *whole hour,* they've filled in the blanks and totaled the page. If the total was less than or equal to their take-home pay, they pronounced it "a budget." The assumption seems to be that a budget is meant to just keep us from overspending. Thus, they have sketched a map to solvency only. If things look like they'll end up in the black, they're satisfied. They have a nice warm feeling in their heart, assuming that, at last, they've finally gotten organized and disciplined. Their glow is short-lived.

Unfortunately, within a few days, their plan is disrupted by the rude arrival of an unexpected bill—the quarterly car insurance premium. By budgeting from a monthly perspective, they overlooked some of the bills that fall due on a quarterly or semi-annually basis. "Well," they think, "that's easy to fix." So they do some minor shuffling, subtracting a little from the clothing and the entertainment category, and "presto-chango" they've pasted their plan back together, and they're still "within budget."

Before long, however, another unexpected expense crops up, and the shuffling process begins again. This time the shuffling reaches levels that would earn admiration in a Monte Carlo casino. Shortly thereafter (this interval ranges anywhere from two minutes to a couple of days), this fragile ruse is exposed for what it is and, with a combination of frustration and relief, they hurl their "Monthly Budget" into the trash and declare themselves "finished with budgets!"

If something akin to this Chaplinesque scene has been your experience with budgets up until now, cheer up. The fact is, you've never actually tried the real thing.

Are you ready for a breakthrough in thinking on the subject of budgets? Here it is: A budget is not the brakes, *it's the steering wheel.* Too often we think of a budget as merely the way to stay solvent. We suppose that its purpose is to *prevent* overspending. A budget is more than the road to solvency; it's the expressway to reach the specific goals and dreams we desire.

With that in mind, we can identify three fatal flaws in the typical budget scenario:

1. Budgeting in the wrong time interval.
2. Beginning at the wrong end of the process.
3. Not devoting enough time at the outset to think and plan.

PRINCIPLES OF SUCCESSFUL BUDGETING

Applying the following seven rules for budgeting will help you avoid the flaws and fallacies and put you on a successful track:

1. Define Annual Objectives:

Start your budgeting process by deciding what you want to accomplish in the next twelve months. How much do you want to save? How much debt do you want to retire? What major purchases do you want to make this year? Is this the year you're going to upgrade the computer system? Is this the year you're going to redo the backyard? This part of the budget can be fun, and I hope you'll make it so.

2. Budget from an Annual Perspective:

The tendency to plan from a monthly perspective leads to many pitfalls. People grab a monthly form and make projections on some "average month" that doesn't exist. The problem with that approach is that all months are not created equal. A December is a whole different animal for most of us than, say, a March or an April.

Just as any good business does, a household must budget from a yearly perspective. Look at the year as a whole and develop an annual plan. This approach may take a little more thought at the outset, but it pays off in the long run.

3. Use a Comprehensive Budget Guide:

To create a comprehensive plan you need a comprehensive format or guide. Several excellent software applications provide that benefit. The most famous one is Intuit's "Quicken," but there are several comparable programs that also are very good. You can check your PC magazines and consumer guides to compare their features. If you choose not to go electronic, you can obtain an excellent budget system with an accompanying booklet of instructions from my company. Call 1-800-622-6463, and ask for "The Money Owner's Kit," or visit the Quma Learning website, www.quma.net.

4. Verify the Facts:

Budgeters run into trouble when projecting their expenditures if they "just wing it." Before you start pulling numbers out of the air, look back at your recent spending history. Grab last year's check registers and a large sheet of paper. Make ten or fifteen columns on the paper so you can create expense categories. (The Money Owner's Kit contains sheets made for this purpose called "Disbursement Ledgers" that simplify this step.)

Teaming up with another person speeds the process. One of you reads off the checks and the other posts the amounts. Starting with the first check of the year, the reader reads the payee and the amount, and the poster records the amount in the appropriate column. If, for example, the first check was made to a grocery store, enter the amount in the "groceries" column. If the next check says, "Chevron," enter the amount in the "vehicle/transportation" column. And so on.

If you make a lot of purchases with credit cards, you'll need to use those statements to categorize those expenditures as well. Once the poster gets used to the categories, he or she can make the entries about as fast as the reader can read, and you'll fly through your monthly check statements in less than an hour, and it's worth it.

5. Categorize Expenses by When They Fall Due:

Some of your expenditures come quarterly and some come annually. Take the time to itemize the expenditures that don't come monthly. Several expenditures come once a year, like the summer vacation, Father's Day, and Mother's Day, for example. A good comprehensive budget guide will help you think of and plan for these non-monthly expenditures as well. Don't ignore this rule; it's an important key to your budgetary success.

6. Make Joint Commitments:

You and your partner are stronger as a team than you can be separately. Adopting new habits requires conscious effort until they become ingrained, and it's easier to do that when you support one another. At times, good reasons to deviate from your plan occur. Let that always be a joint decision. Work as a team; strengthen each other with constant communication and mutual commitment.

7. Be Tough:

When you're tempted to break from your plan, rejoice. Think of the temptation as an opportunity to exercise your disciplinary muscle. Every time you're enticed to deviate from your course and you reject the enticement, you grow stronger.

CHAPTER 19

The Wealth Plan
Step 6: Own Only the Essentials

Adam Smith, a respected economic authority of the 18th century, wrote a landmark book titled *The Wealth of Nations*. This book, now over two hundred years old, is considered to be the cornerstone of the free enterprise system. In that admirable work, Mr. Smith stated: "The real price of everything, what everything really costs to the man who wants to acquire it, is the toil and trouble of acquiring it."[1]

With all due respect, Adam Smith was wrong on this matter. *Acquiring* is merely the prologue, barely a snowflake in a Himalayan avalanche of expenses which ensue when one acquires a bunch of mortal possessions.

COUNT ALL THE COSTS

Possessions exact far greater expenditures from their owners than the mere toil and trouble of obtaining them. As a proud owner, you are now responsible for care, maintenance, and upkeep. You must protect and preserve your treasure, otherwise all the effort expended to acquire it in the first place goes for naught. Acquirement is only the wedding. Upkeep and maintenance are the marriage. And few live happily ever after.

You see owners wherever you go. They are the ones with their sleeves rolled up, perspiration pouring off their brows, straining to repair, refurbish, or restore some mute, inanimate, and ungrateful object. They stand there splattered with paint or grease, shelling out more cash to preserve what they shelled out cash to acquire. Sometimes it's difficult to actually determine who owns whom. The owner seems to be the one whose freedom and mobility has been diminished. It is the owner who devotes time before work, after work, on holidays, on days off, and during vacations tending the possessions. It is the possessor who's huffing and puffing, vainly trying to forestall the ravages of disintegration. The possession makes no commotion. It just politely goes ahead and rusts.

All ownership is a form of bondage. I realize you may think me extreme, but consider my point carefully. How much of our life and creative genius is spent taking care of "stuff?" We owners are futilely trying to reverse the course of the irreversible, consuming time and energy in the process—resources that have greater value than the possession. I can't picture myself being all that thrilled looking down on my funeral as someone says, "Well, here's Dennis, who sure took good care of a lot of stuff."

Things in this world do not stay neat, tidy or new; they dilapidate. It's actually a law of the universe. Science calls it entropy, but it comes down to two simple words, *stuff breaks.* Dust it is, and unto dust it is returning.

Do you have stuff? All of it, at this very moment, is breaking down and coming apart. The stage of decomposition is all that varies. Take a look around; everywhere you go you see things falling apart. Think before you go acquiring all that stuff how much time and effort it will take to keep it all in running order.

We've all chuckled at the bumper sticker that states, "He who dies with the most toys wins." Let me add that he also dies first. Some of us are wearing ourselves out, driving ourselves to early graves trying to find happiness by owning ever glossy new toy on the market.

This truth was not lost on the mind of billionaire, H. Ross Perot. He stated to the students of Harvard Business School,

> Just remember, if you make a lot of money, if you go out and buy a lot of stuff—it's gonna break. You got your biggest, fanciest mansion in the world. It has air conditioning. It's got a pool. Just think of all of the pumps

> that are going to go out. Or go to a yacht basin any place in the world. Nobody is smiling, and I'll tell you why: Something broke that morning. The generator's out; the microwave oven doesn't work...Things just don't mean happiness.

Owners are not as deliriously happy as non-owners think they are. They are walking around, muttering obscenities, with burdens of maintenance on their backs. Ownership means responsibility. When that responsibility is for something which is going irreversibly downhill, we do well to keep ownership to a modest level.

OWN ONLY THE ESSENTIALS

I'm not saying that we shouldn't own *anything*—that we shouldn't own our homes, a nice car or two, or some furniture. On the contrary, I'm a strong advocate of home ownership. Definitely: *Own your home!* In fact, go all the way. Don't just pay on it. Own it! Get yourself into a nice comfortable home and get it paid for as soon as you can. But don't go on a vanity trip there either. Avoid being a SITCOM. (You know what SITCOMs are don't you? Single Income Two Children Outrageous Mortgages.) They aren't that funny, and neither are DITCOMs (Dual Income . . .). I know families who are in bondage to a huge house with its huge monthly payment, huge utility bills, huge property taxes, huge insurance costs, and gargantuan upkeep and maintenance demands. No matter how plush, a prison is a prison.

Up to a point, property ownership is wonderful. Just remember that it comes with a *continuous* price tag, and don't get carried away. Keep your balance and your perspective. Own what you *need.* Own some things that you *want,* too. But do not imprison yourself behind walls of material possessions.

RENT THE ACCESSORIES

Count costs, especially when it comes to toys, recreational equipment, and recreational properties. I love Lake Powell, that picturesque marvel on the Utah-Arizona border. As a family, we've spent many pleasant days on a houseboat enjoying its beauty. Lake

Powell has something for everyone. Swimming, fishing, water skiing, mud wrestling—whatever.

For me, it's a carefree place. Parenting is easy there. I can just turn the family loose on the beach without having to worry about a lot of property damage. They can't fracture or destroy anything real costly or expensive. So, I don't have run around shouting, "Don't touch that!" or "Stop that!" or "Be careful, you might break..." or "Watch out, you are going to ruin the..." and, so forth.

I enjoy more peace when not trying to avert disasters by small unskilled hands. At Lake Powell, I relax. My little ones can't sunder the sandstone or break the lake. They can't even stain or soil it much. It is about as sandy as it is ever going to get. All we have to do is pick up and carry off the litter when we leave (and, in that category, we try to go the extra mile).

Consequently, I can enjoy my time and *the people* I love most. I can do that because I am not preoccupied with property damage. I've seen parents turn into boorish wrecks because they just bought a beautiful luxury cruiser and have to protect it all week. (They'd have more fun if they underwent liposuction without anesthesia.) Those lovely boats, so cherished in the show room, become sources of anxiety and tension on the lake. The parents lose sight of their purpose for the family vacation in the first place. They start resenting every movement their children make. "Don't do that, you'll scratch the..." "Stop that, you'll tear the..." "Watch where you are putting your punch, you'll stain the..." ad infinitum (and ad nauseam).

IT'S MR. WEBB'S BOAT (PROBLEM)

So, here's what I do: I refuse to own the houseboat. When I want to go to Lake Powell and spend a week with the family on a houseboat, I pick up the phone, call Mr. Del Webb's company,2 and make a reservation. I mail a deposit and write a date on my calendar. I do not have to worry about tune-ups, or whether the battery is charged. My only worry is whether or not last year's swimming suit still fits. (Hey, Susan, where's the 245 sun block?)

When I arrive at Lake Powell, the friendly folks at the marina provide me with a clean, decently operating houseboat that's gassed and ready for loading. I don't have to drag it behind my car and pray that it stays there until I get to the lake. (I have a friend who was pulling his boat to the lake and saw it pass him on the freeway.)

My way is less exciting; I just have to steer the car I am riding in. I do not have to worry about the boat along the way, or even launch it when I get there.

I then spend a week enjoying Lake Powell with my family with minimal concerns about the wear and tear on Mr. Del Webb's houseboat. We are clean, responsible people, and my children are well mannered. We do not destroy the rented property, but even if we did, I wouldn't have to call Dr. Kevorkian. My worries and financial responsibility would not be overwhelming.

When our holiday comes to a close, we gather what remains of our belongings, thank the folks at the marina, find our car, and drive home. I don't have to vacuum the carpets, wash the boat, disinfect it, or even park it. I just leave it in the water, more or less by the dock there. If a few new scratches show up on the paint, I don't fret, and Mr. Del Webb hasn't yet called to yell at me for smudging the windows. Furthermore, from that point on, all of the joys of ownership are Mr. Webb's to savor for the rest of the year. If that night a freak tsunami should blow through the territory, ripping every houseboat on the lake to micro-particles, such news won't even spoil my next nap.

AND, IT'S NICE TO CHOOSE

We look forward to our family vacations. I love spending some of them, as I said, at Lake Powell; but I also love *not* spending some of them at Lake Powell. Sometimes it's fun to bop over to Disneyland instead. I also love to just stay home with the family and support my children in their various hobbies and activities. Above all, I love being FREE—free to do what feels fun, right, and most desirable at the moment.

I don't want to feel obligated by some toy or possession that I've bought! People who dump big money into boats, cabins and vacation condos often feel pressured to spend lots of extra time "enjoying" those toys in order to get their "money's worth." The expenditures haunt them a little. When they'd just like to stay home for the weekend, they can't quite bring themselves to do it. You hear them snarl at their children: "Come on, kids. Get in the car. We're going up to the cabin to have fun," they growl (in their un-funnest voice).

Don't let your decisions about how to spend your time be driven by how you spent your money. I don't know about you, but I want my free time to be *free* time.

DOLLARS AND SENSE

Laying the peace-of-mind issue aside, plowing a ton of money into recreational toys makes little sense. A houseboat is not a small ticket item (in case you haven't noticed). One big enough for my family comes to a sizeable sum—something upwards of $200,000. If I really go on an ego trip, I could easily spend $300,000. To handle my family with spouses and friends, we're not talking about a canoe here. We're talking about Motel 6 on pontoons!

Let's say that I decide to buy a $250,000 houseboat. That's just the sticker price. Let's say that I finance a major portion of it. That adds finance charges and interest costs to my recreation tab. Next comes property tax and licensing. (Such expenses also have the nasty habit of occurring annually thereafter.) These expenses are followed by insurance premiums. Then comes the question of docking or storage. (You don't just let the air out of a houseboat and put it in your pocket. And you certainly would not want vandals mangling your treasure.)

All of this is just a foreshadowing of what is to come. The great law of the universe, Stuff Breaks, now comes into effect. Your gorgeous boat begins a gradual but unmistakable (and irreversible) voyage to rust and dilapidation. Since you are the proud *owner* of all that, "all that" is now your responsibility; and your time, your strength, and your pocketbook are the only weapons you have to counter the corrosion. You soon find that this arsenal cannot match the opposing force; the disintegration happens no matter what.

If you add up the purchase price and all of the aforementioned insults to your wallet and estate, the cost for a couple of weeks at Lake Powell reaches staggering heights. Even if we set aside all the irritating expenses, worries, and distractions, and only consider the principal, the math doesn't favor ownership.

Let's suppose that instead of handing over $250,000 to the boat dealer and money lenders, I just rolled it into a Certificate of Deposit (CD) that paid 7 percent (current rate). My annual after-tax income on the CD would be about $11,700.[3] If each week's rental at Lake Powell cost $5,000, (current rate) I could get two weeks for $10,000. Just the interest on my principal covers the rental. In fact, I'm $1,700 ahead right there, plus I still have my principal working to pay for next year's vacations.

Saving the $1,700 each year, I have a bit more principal generating a bit more interest each year. In twelve years, my boat, if I own it, would be ready for refurbishing, requiring more cash. By not owning it—by renting it when I want it—I'd have over $270,000 and no ulcers. (Think of the money I'd save on Maalox.)

TO BE MORE, OWN LESS

The real issue is not how much one can save or make by owning less, but what one can do or be by owning less. Our mortal span is decidedly brief. What we do with our time outweighs what we buy with our money. By owning only the essentials, you'll have time and more space for who and what really matters.

---

1. Adam Smith, *The Wealth of Nations,* P.F. Collier and Son, New York, 1909, p.36.
2. Actually, Del Webb doesn't own or operate the houseboat franchise on Lake Powell any more. (I think he got tired of all the upkeep too.)
3. Assuming 33 percent tax bracket.

CHAPTER 20

The Wealth Plan Step 7: Own a Low Maintenance Investment Plan

Are we financially free if we're constantly stewing over our portfolio? Are we free if we're riveted to a screen, scouring the Internet, fretting over every blip in the market or the gyrations in penny stocks? Such a picture doesn't match my definition of financial freedom. For this and other good reasons, I emphatically recommend a *low maintenance* investment strategy.

We certainly need and want our money to grow, but we want to accomplish that end without sacrificing the majority of our time and mental effort. Those who spend their life vainly trying to outsmart the market settle for pottage, no matter how much money they handle. A low maintenance investment plan provides ample success while freeing up more time. Ultimately, where we invest is more important than when. And what we do with our time, while the money's working, matters even more.

PREPARING FOR SUCCESS

With money or earthly assets nothing is perfectly safe. No

matter what we do—no matter where we put our money—we can still lose it. Banks, savings and loans, and credit unions have failed and people have lost cash. Insurance companies have failed and people have lost money. Retirement funds have been embezzled or so mismanaged that innocent people have lost their nest eggs. Stocks have become worthless; bonds have defaulted. Gold, silver and diamonds can be lost or stolen. Cattle can die, apartments can burn down (actually, I've wished some of mine *would*), governments and companies can muddle, go bankrupt, or be taken over. Even cash can be stolen, lost or beamed to other galaxies by aliens. (Well, it said so in the *Enquirer*.) Bottom line: In the absolute sense of the word, nothing is absolutely safe. Investment implies risk.

Accepting risk as a given, the question remains, "What do we do with our accumulating savings?" Many factors determine the answer. For one thing, the antics of inflation markedly affect the appeal of any given investment at any given time. When the rate of inflation is increasing, tangible assets are advantageous to own. When the rate of inflation is declining, cash and cash equivalents are better. People who "play the game" flop back and forth with the oscillating swings of the economic pendulum. We're going to respect the impact of inflation without worrying too much about "playing the game." We're going to adopt a strategy that succeeds while acknowledging that the economy will perpetually ebb and flow.

Besides inflation, a host of other factors influence investment decisions, and we'll deal with the more significant ones as we proceed. Let's look at a few key considerations.

KEY NO. 1: GET PREPARED

Preparation precedes power in any field we care to name—from sports and athletics to business. Nevertheless, this essential key goes under-respected and unapplied.

A lot of people get into financial trouble because they launch into the world of investment prematurely. They get greedy, dive into speculative ventures, get strung-out, sell early, and lose money.

First, get strong and unencumbered. Call that your first investment if you wish. Implement the preceding steps in the Wealth Plan. Establish your discipline—live on less than you make, eliminate all debt but your home mortgage, and live by a solid money expenditure plan. Then you are ready to soar.

The second advantage that comes from this key relates to patience. Impatient people seldom prosper in the markets because most investments require a period of time to grow. That's why being solid financially before we enter the fray pays off. If we're in a hurry to generate some cash, hoping our investments will pay off quickly so we can pay bills and head off foreclosures, we're doomed. The adage, "Haste makes waste," holds particular value for successful investors.

KEY 2: DETERMINE THE INVESTMENT HORIZON

The investment horizon is crucial. If you are reading this chapter while lying in bed, half asleep, put the book down and go to sleep. Read this when you are fully alert, because what comes next is pivotal to your investment success.

The foremost decision—the one that drives everything else—is to determine *the length of our investment horizon.* We must decide when we want our money back. This decision precedes every other one and governs all subsequent decisions. Before we can decide where to invest, we must determine how long we can let the money work. For our purposes we're going to say that if we need the money in less than ten years, we have a short-term horizon. If we can let the money work for ten years or longer, we have a long-term investment horizon.

When we get down to investment choices, a fairly finite list exists. New twists crop up all the time, but they are, almost without exception, variations on old themes. Based on Nobel Prize-winning research, focused on the performance of investment vehicles, a very important point comes to light: *The best performing investments for short-term horizons prove to be the poorest for long-term horizons.* And vice-versa.[1] Studying statistics on investment performance compiled by Ibbotson and Associates,[2] and other respected authorities, we discover the reason: The biggest risk factor for short-term investors is volatility—the rapid fluctuation in value. The biggest risk factor for long-term investors is inflation—the erosion of value.[3]

Investments with low volatility prove to be superior in short term horizons, but over the long haul they barely keep pace with inflation. At the same time, investments with moderate to high volatility generally out-pace inflation and provide genuine gain when the investor has a long-term horizon.

Thus, we must be careful to choose the type of investment that corresponds to our time frame. People who pick short-term vehicles for long-term objectives, wind up with disappointing results. Similarly, people who select volatile investments for short-term objectives often suffer losses. So, we're going to use short-term investments for our short-term goals, and use long-term vehicles for our long range goals. Simple. But you'd be surprised how many people don't know or don't heed that simple rule.

Having both horizons at the same time is fine. In fact, most individuals *need* both. If we're just starting our adult years, we need both horizons. We'll probably need money for the down payment on our first home in a few years. At the same time, the money in our freedom reservoir won't be tapped for thirty years or more. So, we'd use short-term vehicles for our down-payment money, and more volatile investments for our retirement money because we want to knock the socks off inflation in the long run.

Even if we're in retirement or on the verge of retirement, we'd be wise to employ both strategies. Some of our money will be needed within the next ten years, and some of it needs to be working hard for the latter part of our retirement.

INVESTING FOR SHORT-TERM OBJECTIVES

In general, our best investment for short-term success is a loan. Not as the borrower—as the lender!! We want to be the one sitting on the lending side of the table, contracting with someone reputable, allowing them to use our money for a while at a good, solid interest rate. Here are three time-proven ways to lend money:

1. Certificates of Deposit

They may not be glamorous, but CDs have a lot to offer investors with a short-term horizon.[4] A CD is a contract between us and a bank or credit union. We agree to deposit (lend) an amount of money for a fixed period of time. For this guarantee, the bank agrees to pay us a higher interest rate than we'd receive in a passbook account, rewarding us for leaving the money untouched for the designated period. We give up a little flexibility in exchange for a better interest rate. (We can, in actuality, withdraw the money any time, but we suffer a heavy penalty for doing so—generally the loss of the interest.)

The longer we tie our money up with the bank or credit union, the higher the interest rate they pay. Usually, for periods longer than one year, the incentive is not worth the restrictions, but that's not always the case. As a general rule of thumb, opt for short maturities (six-month or one-year) when interest rates are low and likely to be going up. Conversely, choose longer maturities (three-year or five-year) when interest rates are high and likely to be going down. The definition of "high" and "low" is somewhat arbitrary and you can set your own scale, but for CD purposes "high" generally means eight percent or better. Whenever we can make eight percent or more, guaranteed, we shouldn't disdain it.

Favor federally insured institutions. Federally insured means that an agency of the U.S. government, the Federal Deposit Insurance Corporation (FDIC), stands behind all deposits of $100,000 or less. Even if the bank defaults, the agency stands behind our account and we'll get all of our money back. Banks and credit unions that aren't federally insured usually have a private insurer. Even if they offer a better rate, we're wiser to go with the federally insured institutions.

2. Money Market Mutual Funds

Money Market Mutual Funds (MMMF) are convenient and flexible, and allow us ready access to our money while it earns a decent rate of interest. MMMFs (not to be confused with money market accounts from banks and credit unions) are a way of obtaining a rate of return comparable to a $1,000,000 CD. In essence, we're pooling our money with other small investors to gain the same return the "big investors" get. Hence the name "mutual" fund.

Money market mutual funds can be obtained from brokerage firms (like Morgan Stanley Dean Witter, Merrill Lynch, etc.) or by dealing directly with one of the fund families (like Fidelity, Vanguard, American Century, etc.) or through your independent financial adviser.

Money market mutual funds offer several advantages:

1. Higher Yields. Most MMMFs compound daily. The money is invested in short term loan instruments with very short maturities. These funds outperform passbook savings by a good margin and usually compare favorably to the longer CDs.

2. Low Fees. Ordinarily, MMMFs waive their front-end commissions (sometimes referred to as "loads"), but that's not always the case. They generally exact only a modest management fee.
3. Check-Writing Capability. Many MMMFs offer a check-writing option that allows us to write checks and draw from the fund as long as the check amount is $250 or more.[5] We can't use this as a household checking account, but it's a great place for our emergency fund. This provision makes an MMMF even more liquid than a passbook and we make more interest.
4. Immediate Liquidity. We can withdraw our entire fund at any time by simply writing out a check for that amount.
5. Safety. MMMFs are among the most stable and dependable investments out there. The risk is minimal, especially in the funds which specialize in federal paper.

Several types of money market funds exist. Each invests (lends) your money in a different category of short-term instruments. One type will invest only in corporate notes. Another invests only in federal government bills with short to ultra-short maturities, and others invest only in municipal instruments. Each may have advantages or disadvantages, depending on your situation. Your investment adviser, accountant or broker can answer your questions and discuss the pros and cons with you.

3. Treasury Bills

Treasury bills, often called T-bills, are about the safest way to invest for short term purposes. You're lending your money to the U.S. government, which is as safe as it gets on this planet. For people in high tax brackets, and especially for those who live in states with high personal income tax rates (like California and New York), they offer the added advantage of being exempt from state and local taxes.

T-bills are issued in maturities of 13 weeks, 26 weeks and 52 weeks. You buy them below the face value at what is called "the discount rate," and when they mature, you receive the face value on the bill. When held to maturity, your profit amounts to the difference between the face value and the amount you paid for them. You can sell your T-bills before they reach maturity at market rates, but you often incur a brokerage commission that cuts into your profits.

To invest in Treasury Bills, set up a "Treasury Direct" account. By doing so you avoid paying commissions. For more information on how to establish a Treasury Direct account, or on T-bills in general, call the Bureau of the Public Debt at (202) 874-4000, or better yet, visit their website, www.publicdebt.treas.gov. This site is well designed and full of valuable information.

SUBDUE YOUR PASSIONS

Unless interest rates have risen to atypical heights, or sunken to uncommon lows, the returns we receive on short-term investments are rather conservative. The returns generally range from five to eight percent. Considering the surety of the growth and the low risk involved, especially when inflation rates are modest, these are acceptable rates of return. Don't reject them out of pride or lust for bigger returns.

In rare periods, returns have been higher than eight percent and sometimes they have dipped below five percent. Such conditions are deviations from the norm, and are not likely to last long. If rates of return on such conservative investments soar, take full advantage of those unusually favorable conditions, but don't be surprised when they fall back to historical norms. Always keep in mind that *the return of your principal is more important than the return on your principal.*

---

1. Harry Markowitz, *Portfolio Selection: Efficient Diversification of Investments,* John Wiley and Sons, 1959; Yale University Press, 1970; Basil Blackwell, 1991; *Mean-Variance Analysis in Portfolio Choice and Capital Markets,* Basil Blackwell, 1987, 1989, 1990 paperback; "A More Efficient Frontier," *The Journal of Portfolio Management,* May 1999.
2. Ibbotson and Associates. www.ibbotson.com.
3. Markowitz, ibid.
4. For additional free information on Certificates of Deposit, contact the US Securities and Exchange Commission. 800-732-0330.
5. Minimum check amounts vary from fund to fund.

CHAPTER 21

The Wealth Plan Step 7 (Continued): Own a Low Maintenance Investment Plan

If investment returns of five to eight percent don't spin your top, and you say, "I've got to have a better return than that," you can do it. But you'll need to shift your investment horizon and mean it. Returns of 10 to 12 percent are realistic—but not in a short-term context.[1]

INVESTING FOR LONG-TERM OBJECTIVES

When we shift from a short horizon to a long one, we also shift our basic investment premise—we shift from loanership to ownership. We've got to keep the ravages of inflation in mind and own something that's going to go up in value over time and out-pace inflation. Sounds easy enough, and famed political humorist, Will Rogers, made it sound even easier: "Take all savings and buy some good stock and hold it until it goes up, then sell it. If it don't go up, don't buy it."

The concept is simple, but finding something to buy at a reasonable price that will keep going up can be a whole lot trickier than it sounds. The stock market tends to go up *over time.* However, it doesn't just go up and up and up. On its way to up, it goes through a good number of downs too. Both the stock market and the general economy have had, and will continue to have, their fevers and their chills. People who try to time the market—attempting to sell just before a chill and buy just before the next fever—are humbled in no time at all. However, history shows that investing in the stock market *for long periods* of time proves to be very profitable, trouncing inflation soundly.

So, if you seek returns greater than eight percent, you should look to the American stock market, and buffer the risks by committing to a *long-term* approach. Success depends on harnessing time not timing.

BROAD-SPECTRUM MUTUAL FUNDS

When considering a simple, low-maintenance approach for long-term objectives, broad-spectrum mutual funds are hard to beat.

Let me briefly clarify that in this chapter the term "mutual funds" will refer to stock funds also called "equity funds," because they invest in stocks (as opposed to bond funds that invest in bonds). "Broad-spectrum" means that the investment objective of the fund is to spread its holding across the breadth of the economy, buying stocks from multiple sectors of the economy. In effect this broad-based approach allows you to invest in America, participating in the overall prosperity. These funds have had an impressive success record over many decades, and they offer a number of solid advantages for our long-term money.

First, we enjoy instant diversification. If we buy one or two individual stocks, our profits rise and fall based on the fortunes of those two companies. Our risk is higher. Because mutual funds buy stock in many companies (an average of 90 to 150), when we buy shares in a single mutual fund we actually own shares in dozens of companies. One of the advantages of mutual fund investing is that we spread our risk over multiple entities.

Broad-spectrum mutual funds take that good idea one step further. They not only invest in multiple companies but they invest in multiple sectors of the economy. By contrast, some funds specialize, investing in a narrow sector of the economy, and are sometimes called "niche" or "sector" funds. Narrow-spectrum or niche funds prove to be much more erratic and volatile. Although they invest in many companies, all of the companies do about the same thing, and when that industry prospers those funds climb. Conversely, when that industry lags or falters, nothing offsets the downturn and those funds struggle.

Broad-spectrum mutual funds essentially invest in America,[2] an arena with an unparalleled history of safety and prosperity,[3] because the money is spread across the breadth of the economy. Since bad news for one sector can actually be good news for another, these funds have something going for them in all seasons. When one or two sectors are doing poorly, a couple of other sectors are usually booming. Overall, year in and year out, America tends to prosper and the money invested across the spectrum also prospers. Even during so-called "general recession," we can expect one or two areas of the economy to grow. During those times our fund may not be soaring, but at least it won't be plummeting to the basement like an elevator with a broken cable. Broad diversification buffers risk.

The second big advantage to mutual fund investing is that we can expect attractive long-term returns. A historical overview reveals the following significant points:

1. Over ten-year periods, stock funds outperform bank products such as passbook savings accounts, money market deposit accounts, and CDs.[4]

2. Over ten-year periods, stock funds outperform bonds.[5]

3. Over 15-year periods, stock funds beat inflation by seven percent or more.[6]

4. The longer we hold stock funds, the greater the likelihood of earning compounded annual growth of 12 to 15 percent. Even holding stock funds for ten to twelve years has historically averaged 10.5 percent per year.[7]

Other advantages to mutual funds include low-cost professional management (we pay a small percentage of our account value to the fund manager), low cost personal management (monitoring our fund is quick and simple), and modest minimums to start (some as low as $250 or $500).

The final advantage is *liquidity.* Mutual funds are easy to convert to cash. Most mutual funds are "open-ended," meaning when we invest in a fund, the fund issues new shares. When we want to sell, the fund buys the shares back. No questions asked. We don't have to have somebody willing to buy when we want to sell in order to move on, as we would with individual stocks.

Let's conclude this overview of mutual funds by noting an observation by Peter Lynch, a well-respected Wall Street figure: "Nobody who needs their money in one or two years should be in stocks or stock funds. But if you have a long term investment horizon, a well-selected portfolio of stock funds is bound to prove a winner."

ANOTHER ALTERNATIVE

Given the solid advantages that mutual funds offer, and the minimal maintenance required to monitor them, a well-designed portfolio usually has a solid foundation of two or three mutual funds. After weighing the compelling advantages of funds-only investing, many people have gone that route, and it's hard to argue with their logic or their success. I personally do not know of a single case where the investor fared poorly by following that strategy. Most have, in fact, done extremely well, although we'll always find someone looking a gift-horse in the mouth, saying, "I could have done a lot better if I'd bought Intel at six."

Another profitable alternative exists. I can cite a couple of very successful investors who don't own a single mutual fund.[8] Their choice involves more preparation and more time initially, because they take on more of the role that the fund manager plays with mutual funds. But once established, it too can be fairly low maintenance while providing very healthy long-term gains.

We'll begin with the basics and work our way up.

THREE CARDINAL RULES OF INVESTING

Before you run off to invest your hard earned savings, let's look at three very valuable rules. Even if you consider yourself a seasoned investor, you do well to remind yourself of these time-proven precepts:

1. Always Invest With Your Own Money

Borrowed money does not have the same meaning or value as earned money. You do not take the same pains to look before you leap and that lack of caution can be costly. People who invest with their own money tend to ask tougher questions, look a little deeper, and investigate a bit more thoroughly before they jump—all of which bodes well for better results.

2. Always Invest Based On Your Own Knowledge

Before you put your money in any investment, become knowledgeable in that investment and that market. That point can't be emphasized enough.[9] Although you may be revved up about jumping into mutual funds, you need to educate yourself on the specifics of the market and the methods—information that extends beyond the scope of this book.

Take classes, read books, gain knowledge specific to the type investing you choose to pursue. Do not, because of mental laziness, turn your money over to a professional or an expert and say, "Tell me what to do." Align yourself with reputable advisers in the field, and *collaborate* with them by being a knowledgeable investor. A good adviser can help you work out an investment philosophy and strategy suited to your goals and situation, and the more informed you are the better things turn out for all concerned. Again, the point of life is to become strong and independent. We don't see dependency rewarded very often—especially over the long run. If you expect real success, you must take responsibility for your investments and investment choices, and coupling that with experienced pros who can assist you along the way makes a world of sense.

3. Keep Control

Nobody will take better care of your money than you will. Nobody will act in your best interest as consistently as you will. The financial literature is full of sad examples about people who were too naïve or lazy to make their own decisions. They threw their money to the first "salesperson" who came along and said, "Here's my money. Invest it for me, and call me when I'm rich," and lived to regret it.

Your first responsibility is to become knowledgeable yourself, and your second is to exercise patience and good judgment in selecting competent, reputable advisers.

ADVISERS HELP

Select advisers and accountants as you would a brain surgeon—check their credentials, background, and reputation among their colleagues. Don't rush the process. Ask around. Check with the Better Business Bureau about the company or firm. If your prospective adviser works for an established company, find out how long he or she has been with the firm. Find people with proven performance. Talk to people who have used the adviser's services for several years. If they're still happy over a reasonable period of time, that tells you a lot.

When you look for a brokerage, choose one that's insured by the Securities Investor Protection Corporation (SIPC), another agency of the federal government.[10] Similar to the FDIC, this agency insures your account against loss, if the brokerage should go out of business or become insolvent. Accounts are insured up to $100,000 in cash and up to $400,000 in other assets. Obviously, the "insurance" does not apply to the performance of the assets in the account. If you buy a stock that goes down and you sell, you lose money. (I know of no insurance to cover the risk of investing.)

Accountants and professional investment advisers are very valuable members of your team. In most cases they're indispensable. They can definitely help you form a winning game plan, but you must stay involved. Reputable professionals in the field offer crucial expertise in the following areas: (1) Investment perspectives and advice based on years of experience (a key qualification to look for as you pick advisers); (2) Updates on new laws and government policies; (3) Company and industry data, research and analysis; and (4) Invaluable assistance with tax issues and estate planning, to mention but a few. Assemble a team with the best players possible and stay informed and educated.

THE CALPURNIA PRINCIPLE

If you're familiar with Roman history, or at least William Shakespeare's rendition of it, you'll recognize the name Calpurnia. Calpurnia was Julius Caesar's wife. It was she who received the dark forebodings regarding Caesar's fateful trip to the senate. Her dreams in the night were fitful and she awoke with a warning for her husband, urging him to forgo his appointment that day. Had mighty Caesar heeded his partner, he would have lived past the Ides of March, averting his assassination at the hands of Brutus and Cassius.

In any given partnership or marriage, one partner tends to take the lead in investment matters, and that's fine. But, I firmly recommend that you work as a team, and never proceed with any investment unless you have consensus between the two of you. This principle, which I've dubbed the Calpurnia Principle, if applied, will prevent many investment regrets. More than once, I've witnessed instances where one partner wanted to dive headlong into a venture, but the other had major misgivings. Those "mixed feelings" turned out to be warnings, and when heeded, the partnership avoided a painful setback. The converse also held true. Major blunders resulted when one partner stubbornly pursued a course contrary to the strong reservations of the other partner.

As with any rule, we can find exceptions, but they are few, and I personally cannot think of one exception in my own experience or that of my acquaintances. Strong, united teams beat individual players in virtually every case.

---

1. John C. Bogle, *Bogle on Mutual Funds,* Irwin Professional Publishing, Burr Ridge, Illinois, 1994, pp. 3-23.
2. Excepting, of course, the funds that invest in a menu of foreign companies and/or markets. Such funds are technically "broad-spectrum" (in that they invest in multiple industries) but they are usually referred to as "Global" or "International" funds.
3. J.P. Morgan remarked to his heir, "Remember, my son, that any man who is a bear on the future of this country will go broke." December, 10, 1908. Bill Adler with Bill Adler, Jr., *The Wit and Wisdom of Wall Street,* Dow Jones-Irwin, Homewood, Illinois, 1985, p.46.
4. Ibbotson Associates, *Stocks, Bonds, Bills and Inflation,* Chicago, IL, 2000. See also www.ibotson.com
5. Ibid.
6. Ibid.
7. Bogle, Ibid.
8. I personally do not concur with them. I have a good layer of mutual funds in my portfolio.
9. In the next chapter we will expand on this point.
10. Most brokerage houses—both full-service and discount—are insured by the SIPC, but it pays to verify that fact before you make your decision.

CHAPTER 22

The Wealth Plan Step 7 (Continued): Own a Low Maintenance Investment Plan

IN SEARCH OF "THE SYSTEM"

Since the beginning of the twentieth century, "systems" for beating the market have flourished—a new one coming along just in time to replace the "old" one that failed to live up to expectations.[1] We have no shortage of them now. Our discussion of the stock market and long-term investment vehicles concludes with several formidable principles to add to your stock market savvy.

You may be surprised to know that I believe that a system for excelling in the stock market actually exists. It's just not very stylish or attractive to people in a hurry to make a quick and slick killing in the market. It centers on taking full responsibility for applying the three cardinals rules of investing, and performing the homework and study needed to find genuine bargains—the very thing the people who are looking for the fast formula to big bucks want to avoid.

I didn't invent the system; it's been around a lot longer than I, which brings me to the first point:

Don't look for the latest fad, look for the longest fad.

If we're looking for "a system" to follow, it'd better be an old one, otherwise we're just taking someone's word at face value. How can we really tell if a principle holds true over the long haul? Well, if it's gone ahead and proven itself by actually holding true over the long haul![2] No test serves us better for separating the sages from the soothsayers than the proverbial test of time.

If we're looking for a role model on this principle, we can't do a whole lot better than Warren Buffett. Not only has *he* been around for several decades, consistently demonstrating way-above-average investment success year after year, but he plainly declares that his methods are not his own. He's been employing tried and proven principles that he learned from his mentors and role models[3]—people who also enjoyed exceptional success over long periods of time before him.[4] Whenever we can go back and cite two or three generations of successful practitioners and proponents of a system, we're on to something.

PRINCIPLES OF "THE SYSTEM"

Warren Buffett's statement, "I buy on the assumption that they could close the market the next day and not reopen it for five years," captures the essence of at least four principles that every serious investor should thoroughly understand.

1. IN the Market, Not ON the Market

Successful investors understand the crucial difference between making money *IN* the stock market, and making money *ON* the stock market. The vast majority of folks thrashing around in the stock market call themselves investors, but they aren't. They are prospectors and gamblers. Investors use the market to form partnerships with businesses, and gamblers use the market to place a bet.

The word "invest" comes from a Latin root meaning "to clothe" or "to surround," implying that an "investor" furnishes something of value (money) to improve the status of the thing being "clothed" (supplying a means to create more growth). For this service, the investor receives value in return—a share of the ensuing profits. The term "investment" connotes an element of partnership. To a prospector, that's all a bunch of rubbish. They're just after a quick buck, and the method doesn't matter. If the transaction happens to produce no value or it hurts someone else...well, that's tough.

Investors use the market to join the free enterprise system without having to start a business on their own. This is how the "little guy" can enjoy some of the prosperity while limiting risk.[5] To a certain degree whether the market itself is up or down, or is about to move up or down, is meaningless to a smart investor. They look at the market *as a market*—the place to obtain some ownership of a well-run business.

One of Warren Buffett's most provocative and instructive statements makes this point, "For some reason, people take their cues from price action rather than values...The dumbest reason in the world to buy a stock is because it's going up."[6]

Mentally, prospectors are so far removed from that kind of thinking, it's hard to find an apt analogy. Their casino-mentality dwells on only one thing: timing the direction of a stock or of the market itself. In many respects the particular stock is actually irrelevant to a prospector. They prowl around until some letters on the board catch their eye (IBM, GTE or Beta Theta Pi—it really doesn't matter). Once they spot a stock that's bobbing up and down, they bet on one of the swings. What that particular company actually does is pretty much irrelevant, whether it's led by a group of honest, hard-working managers doesn't enter, how long it's been profitable or how long it's likely to generate profits in the future is superfluous information. Annual reports and financial data are not only impertinent but downright annoying.

Prospectors try to make money *on* the market. Sound investors make money *through* or *in* the market. Buffet explains, "If we find a company we like, the level of the market will not really impact our decisions. We will decide company by company."[7] Closely related, but still distinct from the first principle, is the second:

2. Own Companies Not Stocks

Successful investors are not *playing* the stock market. They're not even in the market; they're *in business*. They study a business thoroughly, and when they discover an exceptional company at an exceptional price, they don't bet on it, they buy into it or join it. They're not trying to figure out which way the company's stock *price* might move in the next few hours. They're studying the company itself. John Maynard Keynes has been credited with the statement, "Don't try and figure out what the market is doing. Figure out a business you understand and concentrate."[8] Warren Buffett confirms that approach: "The market is there only as a reference point to see if anybody is offering to do anything foolish. When we invest in stocks, we invest in businesses."[9] These words are coming from incredibly successful investors, who're sharing an incredibly valuable insight.

Sound investors are not in a hurry. They slow down and study the fundamentals of a company. They look for strong leadership at the top, a proven track record of performance, consistent annual growth and profits, solid and sustainable margins, staying power in their field. They seek to know the company inside and out—literally. They're not only interested in what the company does to make profit, along with its unique selling features and market advantage, they also study the company's competition, and the overall potential of its industry.

When they buy, they buy ownership in the company, not just "stock." They buy *because* they're convinced that the company has long term growth potential in a solid market and that it's the best in its field with a high likelihood of being able to sustain their competitive advantages. And they buy that company *when* they think that it's underpriced in the market—that the current selling price is well below that real value of the stock. All that's required to accomplish that is a little patience, a bit of study and a modicum of (here's that word again) discipline.

Holding a hit-and-run mentality, prospectors can't even sit still long enough to *read* a quarterly report. They're feverishly betting on the next couple of clicks on the ticker. And as soon as they've hit, they're ready to run. These people are as equally at home in Las Vegas as they are on Wall Street.

The opposite holds true for an *investor.* Most of them are not buying into a company so they can dump and run at the first glimmer of profit. They buy into a company with the idea that they may never sell, or at least not for a long time. They buy and hold. They buy a portion of a good company with significant long-term growth potential when it's selling below its true value, and that's why they make healthy profits in the long-term context.

So in terms of our objective to have a low maintenance investment plan, you see that time and commitment are required up front—to do the research, but once that's done, our monitoring duties are not onerous. For the most part, after we've bought, we're holding and holding and holding.

And, closely related, but still distinct from the first two principles, is the third:

3. Don't Fall for the Head Fakes

Have you heard about Beta? It's "an important measure of a stock's volatility in relation to the Standard & Poor's 500."[10] Are you up on Moving Average? It's a way "to gain insight into the direction of a stock. When the short-term average moves above the long-term average, it's considered a buy signal. When the short-term average is below the long-term average, it's considered time to get out."[11] Are you familiar with the Zacks Consensus? That's a quick way of summarizing analyst recommendations on a given stock. And my final question, guess how many of these heady investment tools do investors of the stature of Warren Buffet and Philip Fisher[12] use when they make investment decisions? Zip. Nada. Zero.

The reason sound investors sweep most of the quick analysis aside is because it doesn't drive to the heart of the matter—the things that really determine whether this is not just a good stock but a good business. The factors that deal with price trends I call "head fakes." This expression is an old baseball term referring to a pitcher's way of deceiving a base runner. A lot of the "tools" used by investors fill their heads with detail leading to false confidence or undue worry. What they don't do is give real information about the business.

One of the timeless pearls to glean from Philip Fisher warns, "Don't be influenced by what doesn't matter." So *how can we tell* what matters and what doesn't? Here's my rule: Anything that pertains to the *direction* of the stock price, where it's been or where it's going is non-information. It muddies the water, clouds our judgment and confuses the real issue. As we've already learned, investment giants never invest on that basis—they're not investing in the direction of the stock price, they're investing in the company. Hence things like the stock's price history and price target are red herrings. The price of a stock is a function of its current popularity, not value.

Our goal is actually to find strong companies that are unloved and rejected by the masses—to find a company with strong, proven management and solid fundamentals that's become unpopular with the lemmings in the market.

Two quotes from Warren Buffett will put the period at the end of this paragraph: "You can't buy what is popular and do well." "Great investment opportunities come around when excellent companies are surrounded by unusual circumstances that cause the stock to be misappraised."[13]

4. Value Over Price

A law of equity prevails in the universe. The adage, "nature abhors a vacuum," implies that nature always seeks (and eventually achieves) equilibrium. Good investing profits from this law.

Undervalued stocks make money in the long run. If we find a good company with reputable management that's somehow out of vogue with the "voters" in the market, it's time to buy and hold. Time and all other corrective forces in the universe are on our side. That company's stock will eventually attain its fair value, as the market comes to acknowledge what it previously misinterpreted, and our investment will pay off. Anytime we can legally and ethically buy $1 of value for less than $1, we're sure to come out ahead.

Again Buffett confirms the principle, "If the business does well, the stock eventually follows."[14] Also, "It doesn't have to be rock bottom to buy it. It has to be (1) selling for less than you think the value of the business is, and (2) it has to be run by honest and able people. But if you can buy into a business for less than it's worth today, and you're confident of the management, and you buy into a group of businesses like that, you're going to make money."[15]

The old adage, "Price is what you pay; value is what you get." ought to become the watchword of every investor. Value is the target, and price is only a factor in that calculation. Obviously, tremendous companies can have over-priced stocks, and buying them after everyone else has jumped on the bandwagon would be folly. But even that tactic would be better than buying into a poorly run company with bad fundamentals just because it's selling at a price we can afford and it's been moving upwardly over the past two weeks.

PRINCIPLES, PRACTICES AND PRIMERS

Near the end of the twentieth century, technology stocks soared. People were making money no matter when they bought some of the market darlings. Many of these companies were newly emerging "dot.com" companies that were very difficult to evaluate in terms of the traditional criteria. I had a gentleman at one of my seminars say, "looks like there's a new era in investing and none of the old rules apply any more." I thought to myself, "we'll see." By the middle of the year 2000, headlines in the financial sections were sporting headlines such as, "Old Guidelines Not Antiquated After All," as the NASDAQ[16] ran into extremely turbulent waters. In the long run, time always tells.

My purpose throughout this book has been to encourage each of us to establish firm financial foundations, reaffirming solid principles and practices in our day-to-day living, and avoiding the fads and fallacies that siphon wealth. From this platform of preparation, we develop the mind-set and muscle to invest wisely and well. Value investing has not gone out of style nor will the principles undergirding it.

---

1. I suspect that the search for "the system" goes back earlier than that, probably to the day after the first stock market was formed, but I haven't dedicated the time to verify that suspicion.
2. The same holds true for investment "texts." In general, the older they are the better. If an investment text is strong, it holds its value over time. Three investment texts meet this criterion: *The Intelligent Investor,* by Ben Graham; *Common Stocks and Uncommon Profits,* by Philip A. Fisher; and *Bogle on Mutual Funds,* by John Bogle. Although Bogle's book is of fairly recent vintage, Bogle is not. He wrote this book—the best book ever written on mutual fund investing, in my opinion—after a long and illustrious career as the head of the well-respected Vanguard Group of Investment Companies. These three books merit your study. I strongly recommend them.
3. Buffett credits his success to the philosophy and methods taught by Ben Graham. "Next to my dad," says Buffett, "Ben Graham had more impact certainly on my business life than any individual."
4. Janet Lowe, *Warren Buffett Speaks: Wit and Wisdom from the World's Greatest Investor,* John Wiley & Sons, Inc., New York, 1997, pp. 88-93.
5. An investor can't lose more than he or she puts it. Hence the risk is limited.
6. L.J. Davis, "Buffett Takes Stock," *The New York Times* Magazine, April 1, 1990, p.16.
7. Lowe, p. 96.

NOTES

8. Robert Lenzner, "Warren Buffett's Idea of Heaven," *Forbes 400,* October 18, 1993, p.40.
9. "Faces Behind the Figures," *Forbes Magazine,* January 4, 1988.
10. *Money Central Investor,* Glossary, msn.com, "Beta".
11. Ibid., "Moving Average".
12. See endnote 2 above. Fisher's book, *Common Stocks and Uncommon Profits* has been around since 1957 and it's still one of the finest investment books around. This one's a classic that has passed the test of time with flying colors.
13. Brett Duval Fromson, "Warm Tips from Warren Buffett," *Fortune Magazine,* December 19, 1988, p. 33.
14. Maria Malloy, "Behemoth on a Tear," *Business Week* Magazine, October 3, 1994.
15. Warren Buffett, *Nightly Business Report,* PBS, December 13, 1994.
16. An exchange heavy with technology stocks.

CHAPTER 23

The Wealth Plan Step 8: Own an Expanding Income

The Abbotts are feeling great these days. Financially, they have never felt stronger. They have accumulated $35,000 in their savings account—the largest reservoir they've ever had. Their income is far from lavish, but they are living within their means and enjoying a respectable lifestyle. The future looks even brighter. Their income recently increased, and the prospects for future increases appear virtually certain. They feel solid.

The Babbotts are feeling uneasy. They are weighed down with financial concerns. They, too, live comfortably and prudently. However, their employment situation is unsettled. Their employer is cutting back drastically. There have been layoffs recently, and rumors abound about more to come. The Babbotts have $235,000 in savings, but facing the specter of unemployment, they know their savings could disappear quickly. They feel vulnerable.

The Abbotts feel confident and positive with $35,000 in the bank. The Babbotts can hardly sleep at night with more than six times that much. What's the moral of the story? Reservoirs alone do not provide financial security. Wealth is relative, and financial security has more to do with trends than amounts. Wealth is best viewed as a monetary *flow*—a complete watercourse *system.* Not just the river, nor just the reservoir, nor just the dam, it's the entire system, rainfall to faucet, supplying a continual flow of the indispensable fluid that sustains life.

A life-sustaining river system can't exist without a sturdy dam to exert control over the resource. In financial terms, the dam is your budget and your savings plan. It is founded on the bedrock of your self-control and discipline. Eliminating your debts plugs the leaks in the dam and solidifies the system's strength. If you do all that, you will create a reservoir.

When you have a well-constructed dam with little or no leakage, and a handsome reservoir filling in behind it, you are ready to go back and tend to the river. Once the control system is in place, everything that follows depends on the size of the river itself. Two things determine the flow of a river: the amount of rainfall and the size of the watershed. Increasing either one of these factors enlarges the volume of the river and the rate at which your reservoir fills.

RULES FOR A RIVER

Here are the three fundamental rules for creating a mighty financial river:

1. Labor at something you love.
2. Stay focused and invest in yourself.
3. Solve other people's problems.

Labor at Something You Love

Take this quiz:

1. When you are at work do you find yourself watching the clock?
2. Do you "live" for evenings, weekends, and vacations?
3. Do you tend to pursue exciting, even dangerous, hobbies?
4. If you inherited a fortune, would you quit your job?
5. If you knew you were going to die in three years, would you leave your current profession or occupation?

Those who answer "yes" to these questions have a low likelihood of ever realizing financial success. Worse than that, they are wasting their lives. Forgive my bluntness, but if you are not engrossed by your life's work, your dreams of an abundant income stream will not come to pass.

Many people think they will find happiness in leisure and recreation. Not so. Service begets joy, and fulfilling work is the elixir of life. Robert Lewis Stevenson stated, "If a man loves the labor of his trade, apart from any questions of success or fame, the gods have called him."[1] True, we need a share of diversion and relaxation, but study after study shows that people who love their work live longer, have less disease, and make tons more money. People who love what they do, seldom have to "get away from it all." They're *doing* what they love to do, enjoying the hours of their life, instead of counting them. Even going on vacation is kind of a bother, because what they really want to do is back home. And because they love what they do, they do it well and unconsciously add that magical element called *quality* to their work.

JOHN SERVES

Sometimes defining or describing value can be difficult, but people recognize it when they see it, and they want it. They will even pay more money to get it. Many intangibles factor into the perception of value—things that are not even necessarily part of the product itself. Often it has something to do with the "personal touch" and the extra effort when it comes to service.

I own a car. Generally it is a dependable car, but once in a while it needs some help. When it comes to repairs and maintenance, I want value. Maybe it's paranoia, but at times in the past I felt ripped-off when I've had my car serviced. I had serious doubts about value. And then I met John. John repairs cars; and he gives value. I can feel it. This man conveys that "something extra" every time I take my car in. He's always smiling. Even when he has put in ten hours at work, and you know his body must be exhausted, you still see that smile.

You can tell he loves cars. You sense it when he talks about them. He bubbles over, relating stories and offering careful explanations (including sketches) about how my car is doing and how I need to watch for this and that in the next 5,000 miles or so. Sometimes I get the feeling John likes my car more than I do.

When my car needs help, I don't get a cursory, "It'll cost you $350 bucks to get this one runnin' again, Mac," from John. No sir. John takes me right into the operating room. He wants me to get right under the car, poke my finger into the "blood and guts," to see for myself which part is broken. All the while he's telling me about my options, whether or not a rebuilt part may do, what I can do to "get by for a while," and what will be the best long-term solution. I would never *think* of taking my car to anyone else, and my friends feel the same way. We go only to John, because we want value and service. John gives both, and we give him money in return. John is getting rich. He likes that. But what he *loves* is helping people with their cars.

Stay Focused and Invest in Yourself

Once you have found your life's work, settle in and keep improving your skills. Take note of a key point from a National Science Foundation study on financial high achievers:

> Your work is more likely to make you wealthy than any bet or investment you will ever make. The most profitable place to invest surplus income is in the area which produced the income in the first place...Any investment that helps detach you from work you enjoy and makes you anxious about the future [had] better produce a million dollar profit, because it is costing you the best chance you have, by far, of making a fortune.[2]

Contemporary author, Bill Copeland has written, "If you chase two rabbits, both will escape." Concentrate on expanding the real source of your prosperity: the talent, gift, or service that you're best suited to render. Journalist Walter Lippmann observed, "A man cannot be a good doctor and keep telephoning his broker between patients nor a good lawyer with his eye on the ticker."

I hope that one of your life's goals is to become one of the very best at whatever you do. It is a worthy pursuit, for it fosters continuous improvement and growth as a person. The qualities you obtain as you stretch for excellence allow you to command greater income. You cannot demand or justifiably expect higher wages from your employer or from your society unless your contribution is expanding. This world is not fair in many respects, but I believe that it is equitable on this point. Over the long haul, value extended brings its just compensation in the marketplace.

Study your craft. The doorway to profitability and prosperity is knowledge and expertise. Your mind is what you offer the world. Educate yourself ceaselessly. Read. Study. Some of the best money you will ever spend will be on the development of your mind. The information-intensive age we live in makes this more critical than ever before. Education can no longer be viewed as an event or a stage of life that one passes through. It must be an on-going habit, an integral part of your life and lifestyle. The greater your mental powers, the greater your value to others and to society.

The time and money we spend tinkering in the markets would return far greater rewards if instead we invested in cultivating our minds and our abilities to serve other people.

Solve Other People's Problems

We've all heard the saying, "Wealth went to a person's head." It would have been better said, "Wealth does not go to your head; it *comes from* your head." Ultimately, wealth is a product of the mind. It seldom comes from physical labor. More frequently it stems from vision and creativity. Creative solutions to vexing problems have always been in high demand. Anyone with the insight to come up with an invention, service, or product—something to ease pain, labor, or drudgery—has generally been financially rewarded. Advertisers recognize that the closer the name of a product aligns with the specific problem it solves, the better, as can be seen by the success of products with names like "Easy-Off Oven Cleaner." Such a name leaves no doubt about what the product does or why you might be interested in exchanging cash for it.

The simple truth is that human beings loath exertion, despise problems, and abhor pain. We will avoid any one of these (or any combination thereof) with a vengeance. Anytime someone or something can reduce labor or the cost of labor, demand for that service will emerge. People will gladly pay money to have their problems solved. This is the supreme law of temporal economics.

Calm, clear minds recognize that axiom and capitalize on it. If you want to expand your earning power, expand the vision of yourself in the role of problem solver. The grand question to ask is, "What problems exist in my profession or field of expertise? What problems can I help solve for other people?" Such inquiry triggers the creative juices, producing workable solutions that will lead to a demand for your service. Justly, the reward is proportionate to the magnitude of the problem.

The opportunity to serve frequently comes disguised as "a problem." However, most of us don't look at problems as opportunities to render service. We just wish the problem would go away. Alert people see a problem as a chance to contribute, and they get to work finding a solution. Usually, the first person to find the solution gets the larger reward.

When you're laboring at something you love, investing in your mind, and seeking solutions to other people's problems, something significant happens to you. Your mind is capable of seeing things other people do not see. You heighten your awareness of needs and enhance the likelihood of receiving insights specific to your field of work. Strokes of genius, "lucky breaks," and ingenious breakthroughs don't just happen. Somewhere along the line, someone has put in the hours and effort that resulted in the inspiration.

Through diligence, service, and persistence, you can expand your watershed and seed the clouds. Before you know it, rain is falling. Once it starts, it pours. The rainfall runs to the riverbed. Soon, what was once a brook becomes a robust river, which in turn becomes a mighty torrent. Before long you have an income stream you can scarcely believe, and you will wonder where all that money was hiding during your years of struggle. Like an August thunderstorm, the downpour can come quickly and abundantly. You are never too old, and it's never too late. Once you make the preparations, the rains will come.

---

1. Bill Adler with Bill Adler, Jr., *The Wit and Wisdom of Wall Street,* Dow Jones-Irwin, Homewood, Illinois, 1985, p.18.
2. Srully Blotnick, *Getting Rich Your Own Way,* Doubleday & Co., Inc., New York, 1980, pp. 94, 134.

CHAPTER 24

Own Freedom

I wrote this book because I work with people, teaching and coaching them. For the most part, it's a gratifying experience, but not always. Many people suffer needlessly, squandering their time and their lives. A good portion of their anguish stems from the issue of money.

We need to put money in its place! Although we have enthroned it, money is not king. Money needs to be put back into the ranks of the knights of service—an important contributor to the good of the realm. Many are rightfully alarmed at the deterioration of values, especially among the young people. But from whom do our children obtain their perspectives? From us—from the things we do—not what we preach. We have taught our children that integrity is something we only give lip service to; the *real* bottom line is cash.

We no longer judge people by the nobility of their labors, or the service they render, but solely on the basis of their earnings and possessions. Who gets more respect in our society, an elementary school teacher or a talk show host? A wife and mother is disrespected because she doesn't bring home a paycheck that can be quantified and converted into tangible "symbols of success." Status and respect have become things an accountant determines—a function of a quantity of dollars.

When we judge others by their money, we start judging ourselves by the same hollow criterion. As Jesus of Nazareth pointed out two thousand years ago. "For with what judgment ye judge, ye shall be judged: and with what measure ye mete, it shall be measured back to you."[1] I do not think he meant that just in terms of the hereafter; I believe it also applies to the here and now.

If we judge others by their 1040 form, we begin to judge ourselves by our 1040 form. Our money and our identity become so entwined that they become indistinguishable, and with that fusion comes a loss of value and of values. For example, if we're honest and hard working, but suffer a business reversal, we get depressed because our earnings decline, and we consider ourselves failures. Conversely, if we cut corners, bend the rules of honesty a bit, and take advantage of our neighbor, we get ahead financially. We feel prosperous and the folks next door are also impressed. See the trap?

Thus we set ourselves up for spiritual, moral, and personal debacles. What we *have* becomes confused with what we *are.* Our self-image becomes a mere reflection of our portfolios. One day we wake up and realize that all we have to show for our lives is a list of stocks and properties.

Throughout history, more people have become ensnared in this trap than any other. But it's a prison of our own making. Since it is self-constructed, it can also be self-demolished.

TOTAL FREEDOM

Money is tricky stuff. We can use it to augment our freedom, but most often we wind up diminishing it. We don't intend to; it just works out that way. It all comes back to the critical differentiation between accumulation and acquirement that we made at the beginning of the book. The distinction may at first seem minute, but it makes a vast difference in the end. The by-product of disciplined accumulation is freedom. The by-product of uncontrolled acquirement is bondage. We must be careful not to exchange the greater wealth of life for something lesser. Of all the things to own, own freedom!

Refresh your memory with this definition:

> *Free: (adj.) 1. At liberty; not bound or constrained. 2. Discharged from arrest or detention. 3. Not under obligation or necessity. 4. Independent. 5. Not affected or restricted by a given condition or circumstance. 6. Not subject to external restraint. 7. Unoccupied; available for use. 8. Unoppressed.*[2]

Break loose from the shackles of owing, owning, and earning. Take charge of your monetary life and liberate yourself from the slavery of "just making ends meet." Free yourself from debt and interest payments that sap your strength and future. Free yourself from the cares, expenses, and labors of managing and maintaining a lot of possessions, properties, and "investments." Become *free*, in every sense of that blessed word.

If we'll reduce the relentless acquisition of material things and stockpile some money for a while, that money can start shouldering the work load. Eventually we'll be able to come, or go, or do, or be, much more freely. Money is a lot easier to take care of than most of the things we buy with it. Money is quite maintenance free. We don't have to oil it, paint it, or overhaul any of its parts. Money is carefree—one size fits all, and its color matches anything we wear.

Accumulating money simplifies our life. We're less distracted, think more clearly and can focus better. Our creative genius can flourish, and the ramifications of that are limitless! A free mind is an asset worth seeking.

FREE! SO WE CAN BE, DO AND GIVE

As we take ownership of our money, we become less focused on what's coming in, allowing us to focus on what's going out. When we step off the acquirement treadmill we can take a few deep breaths and look around. We become more aware of the people around us—the people we live with, the people we work with, and the people we could serve. We can become aware of other people's needs because we're not so absorbed in our own.

I have a friend, who, when he heard of terrible fires in a nearby state, decided to contribute himself to the cause. Listening to the radio as he drove to work, he listened to the news broadcasts telling of the large-scale effort needed to control the wild fires. On the spot he decided to do something about it. Because he'd been living a sound financial life he didn't have to restructure the universe or worry about the difference a week's pay would make. He drove to work, took a leave of absence without pay and went to fight the fires.

My friend is a happy person. He has achieved a level of financial stability that allows him the freedom to spontaneously give himself to a good cause, without weeks of strategizing and planning. He is free to go where he wants to be. That is the kind of freedom I want us all to have—the kind of freedom that following the principles and methods outlined in this book will bring.

Ultimately, I'd like us to be in such a position that whatever we did was a gift. I want us to be able to give ourselves—our time, our ideas, our talents, to other people and good causes.

THE READING GRANDFATHER

I know a gentleman who had become successful in many aspects of his life. He held the top position in his company, a large and prosperous concern. He held leadership positions on several notable committees and boards. Yet in the midst of all that, he discovered something wonderful that he'd overlooked.

He was in his fifties, in the third decade of high-paced corporate management and good earnings. One of his grandsons underwent an operation and was confined to a hospital bed for a few weeks. This man decided to take a couple hours off of work one afternoon to visit his grandson. The usual pressures were on him, but he told himself he would take only be a couple of hours and just this one time. He thought perhaps he'd read a story to his grandson, and then get back to the office.

He found his grandson who shared a room with another little boy. The grandfather read a book to the two young boys, and something remarkable occurred. Three human beings had a great time for a couple of hours—together.

Who healed the most that day is hard to say. The busy grandfather went back to the hospital the next day. And then the next. Dozens of books were read. The nurses on the floor started bringing other children into the room to listen and heal. When the demand outgrew the capacity of the single hospital room, a larger "reading room" was provided.

Today the grandfather still pays regular visits on the children at the hospital. His own grandson has long since graduated to the ranks of the healthy, but it makes no difference. There are other "grandsons" and "granddaughters" who love their Reading Grandfather. He's touched a lot of lives. The life he has touched the most is, of course, his own.

Things are not always what they appear. Many subtle ironies exist, and one of them is the principle of giving. It appears to be exporting, but in reality we are importing. The Reading Grandfather found that out. He still runs his company, and he still fights the battles. Over the years he has sat on boards, steered committees, and been a leader. He has been praised, named, and cited. But if you were to ask him, he'd tell you that he's gotten more out of being the hospital's Reading Grandfather than about anything else he's done. He says, "I used to think I was serving when I sat on the board of a charity or was the chairman of a fund raising effort, but I discovered that nothing compares to the one-on-one."

Too many people, either while they are pursuing money or after they get some, want to get away from other people. They insulate and isolate themselves. The more money they make, the more exclusive the neighborhood they want to live in, and the more exclusive the clubs they want to join. They put up fences around their estates, hire guards and build moats. They withdraw from humanity, put up barriers and walls, and then wonder why life seems empty and lonely.

The Reading Grandfather learned that we weren't meant to be isolated. He learned that giving is personal.

A FINAL WORD

In conclusion, one more law of financial freedom deserves your attention. In virtually every culture, there are teachings to the effect that charity is a key to prosperity and an ever-flowing income. I recommend the principle with the added stipulation (which is not my own) that we be generous in our giving and that we give anonymously. Something more than magic occurs when we do.

People who give money with their name attached do well and accomplish much good. Hundreds of thousands of students have been able to further their educations because of generous grants from individuals and foundations that have been set up in the names of prosperous donors. I wish to take nothing away from such generosity. Yet, there is something above that level of generosity: quiet, unassuming charity.

Giving is a delicate art. Nearly as many principles pertain to the dispensing of money as to the obtaining of it. One of the tricky passages to negotiate has to do with dependency. We do no one a favor turning him or her into a dependent when they have the ability to stand

and walk under their own power. Loving parents often cripple their children by excessive generosity to their offspring. The same can happen with people outside the family circle. Assisting people in times of need can be wonderful, but we must be careful not to intervene too early, too often, or with too much. The answer is anonymity.

When we bestow gifts of money on others anonymously, we can do it whenever we want, in any amount we want, to whomever we want. No implied commitments can be assumed, so no one becomes dependent. We're free to give and still free after we give. Everyone benefits.

You will also discover something else—the validity of an ancient principle, "You can't give a crust without receiving a loaf in return." Prove the principle for yourself. Give anonymously and generously, and watch what happens to your own reservoir. You will not go unrewarded, and you too will be able to declare that this principle is real and that it may be the single biggest wealth-producing measure you could ever undertake.

Best of all, you'll find another great source of happiness. From time to time you'll have the sublime experience of hearing someone express thanks to someone other than yourself. When you give anonymously the recipient can only thank God for the gift, and that will bring you even greater satisfaction, because you'll know inwardly that, when all is said and done, that's where the thanks belongs.

Best wishes, my friend, as you seek financial freedom. May your children be blessed with rich parents!

---

1. Matt. 7:2.
2. *New College Merriam-Webster English Dictionary,* Langenscheidt, New York, 1998, page 464.

Index

D

E

F

G

H

I

J

K

L

M

N

O

P

U

V

W

Z